Lightworking with Angels

Book 1

Lightworking with Angels

Book 1

Written by

Ros Place

www.angels-with-ros.com

Published by

Press of Love

www.pressoflove.com

A CIP catalogue record for this book
is available from the British Library
ISBN 978-0-9573249-0-9

Published by Press of Love www.pressoflove.com

Final editing by Jan Jury

Angel line drawing by Kate Barker www.katiebarker.co.uk

Sound editing of visualisations by Guy Rigby
www.onewednesday.co.uk

Contents

Dedication

'Lightworking with Angels' is dedicated to my wonderful, handsome, everything Eddie who does so much, so brilliantly and without needing to tell everyone about it. Without Eddie this book could never and would never have been written, and for that and countless other reasons, I love you Eddie from the bottom of my heart.

I would also like to thank our precious sons Zed and Mani for being precisely who they are and for choosing to come into our family. You are our sunshine and rainbows boys, and we love you more than you will ever know.

Foreward for 2023 Edition

Twelve precious years have passed since with my snoozing baby Emmanuel on my lap, I sat and wrote *Lightworking with Angels Book 1*.

It is with a heart full of love and deep appreciation that I share this updated version with you.

Lightworking with Angels Book 1 (2023 Edition) honours the original version of the book with the same cover and just the gentlest of touches here and there. You will find a new Chapter Nine, Your Guardian Angel at the back of this book written with Tressarn.

In 2020, Tressarn, my guardian angel gave me The Channel of Clarity Method, the step-by-step way to channel your guardian angel. Together, Tressarn and I are dedicated to sharing our heartfelt purpose to help as many people as possible to channel their own guardian angels.

You are most welcome to read more about my work with Tressarn and the Channel of Clarity Method at **www.channelofclarity.com**

As you read *Lightworking with Angels Book 1*, you may like to invite into your heart the knowing that your connection with the Angels is a precious and sacred gift that no one and nothing can take away from you.

More than ever, the Angels are reaching out to help us here on our planet. So many beautiful souls are awakening now and with each new awakening comes such hope. People from all walks of life are finding themselves drawn to learn about the Angels and to understand how to live their true purpose in the highest and most positive ways.

With every newly awakened soul, a new light goes on in our world and hope grows.

Thank you for your precious light and thank you for opening your life to Lightworking with Angels.

With love always,

Ros and Tressarn xxx

A Word from the Author

I have been working with the Archangels for a long time now. I cherish, honour, appreciate and value their infinite Love and wise guidance more than words can say. I love their individual energies and auras; I love their beautiful and breathtaking 'other world' colours and light, and the warmth they bring to my heart every time they appear.

If you would like to have your own personal connection and experiences with the Archangels, then they would like to help you, and through my experiences, so would I.

I had been waiting patiently to write '*Lightworking with Angels*' for some time, and it was the early part of my younger son Emmanuel's life that provided me with the opportunity to get started. As my dozing baby lay contentedly across my lap, I connected with the Archangels and began to write.

'*Lightworking with Angels*' will explain how the Archangels can help you in your daily life. It will introduce you to Archangels and show you their role in the Universe. It will explain how the individual auras and specialisms of Archangels Michael, Gabriel, Raphael, Chamuel, Zadkiel and Metatron can help you. By the end of this book you will understand how you can build a strong and lasting connection with the Angelic Realm in your very own perfect and personal way.

The Archangels would like to help you to re-member how to communicate with them and feel their presence. You are loved more than you can possibly imagine, and your capacity to imagine and experience more Love in your life begins right here.

It is my heart's desire and my life's purpose to bring anyone who wishes to be closer to the An-gels, and to benefit from this closeness in the most meaningful ways.

Having a personal connection with the Angelic Realm is possible for *you*. It is not just for a few lucky or 'special' people. Your own communication channel with the Angels will provide you with all of the constant, pure, positive energy and guidance that you seek in your life.

Whenever I read a book, I am always interested in knowing more about the 'person' behind the words - I always have been. I always feel myself wanting to know more about who they *are*, the life they lead, how they came to be where they are in their life. So, I thought it might be interesting to you to hear something about me.

I live with my husband Eddie, and our sons Zed and Mani, in the beautiful countryside of South Devon in England. We love the people and the sea, the freshness and the lushness that surrounds us. It is a place of beauty and also a place of peace.

People often call me 'The Angel Lady' for which I am very honoured and my Angel work has connected me with many, many people throughout the world, all with the same desire – to improve their lives by working with the Angels.

The Angels have always been with me, guiding me and I am honoured to be here as a channel for their Love and guidance. I love to share the Angels' personal messages and I love to see the Angels arrive with their wings full of positive change and improvement which they bring lovingly into people's lives.

I love to help people to develop their own personal connection with the Angels and it is my heart's desire and my life's purpose to bring anyone who wishes to be, closer to the Love and Light of Angels and to benefit from this closeness in the most personal and meaningful ways.

'It is my heartfelt desire that 'Lightworking with Angels' will help you to become more connected to Angels and Archangels, to know that you are always loved more than you can ever imagine and that there are loving, Angelic energies around you right now, who are waiting to help you and ....all you need to do is ask.'

Sending Love, Light and Happiness to You,

Ros and Tressarn xxx

Lightworking with Angels

Introduction

Introduction

'Lightworking with Angels' is a practical book that explains how the Archangels can help you in your daily life. It is a book for everyone, because the Angelic Realm is not open to just a few lucky or special people, but anyone who lives on this earth. Communication with the Archangels is something that *you*, whoever you are, can experience and cherish. Your own communication channel with the Archangels will provide you with all of the constant, pure, positive energy and guidance that you seek.

Archangels are as real as we are.

Just as we are physical - flesh and blood - they are non-physical - Love and Light. They are powerful light beings of pure Love, and it is their Divine Purpose to help you discover a life that fulfils you and brings you happiness and Love. The Archangels can enhance and improve your life in limitless ways, and they can help you to understand how it is you can have the life you *really* want.

'*Lightworking with Angels*' introduces you to Archangels Michael, Gabriel, Raphael, Chamuel, Zadkiel, and Metatron. Each of these wonderful Archangels will help you to remember how to communicate with them, how to strengthen your connection with them and how to feel their presence in your life.

'*Lightworking with Angels*' will show you how to work with the Archangels' individual energies and specialisms, and it will show you how to build a strong and lasting connection with the Angelic Realm.

The Angelic energy, instruction and Love contained in this book will guide you upwards towards the Realm of Angels. You are always loved more than you can ever imagine. There are Angelic energies around you right now, waiting to help you. All you need to do is ask.

Angelic Invocations

An Angelic Invocation is a special request or an invitation to the Angels to be with you. At the beginning of each Archangel chapter of this book, you will find an Angelic Invocation to read which will invite each Archangel to be with you. Each Angelic Invocation sets the tone for each Archangel chapter and I would encourage you to use and enjoy them.

The Angels would like you to know that all you ever need to do is to *ask* them to be with you and they will be – instantly- every time. It is not necessary to always use a special invocation to call any of the Angels to be with you.

The Archangels gave me their invocations to share with you so that you can become more familiar with their individual energies. The Archangel invocations in this book will help you to become more familiar with the individual energy, qualities and colours of each Archangel and build a strong and lasting relationship.

All of the Archangel invocations in this book can be found on my website, with my love and compliments - *www.angels-with-ros.com/book1*

How to Use Your Archangel Invocation

Your Angelic invocation can be used in lots of ways. You can read it out loud from the book or you could record your own voice; you could ask a friend or loved one to read your invocations to you or just hold your book in your hands and feel the energy of the Archangels reach you at the beginning of each chapter.

Whichever way you choose, enjoy your Archangel Invocation and then be still and feel how good it feels to know that they are with you. Regardless of whether or not you can feel the Archangel you have invited – they are there, instantly always, every time and without question.

Just allow yourself the pleasure of knowing that the Archangels are there and with you throughout all the pages of this book.

Enjoy inviting the Archangels to be with you, whenever you would like to feel their Love and energy in your life.

Oracle Cards

There are an incredible variety of Oracle Cards available today. You can find Angel Oracle Cards and Archangel Oracle Cards and hundreds of other different and wonderful types of Oracle Cards. I *love* working with Angel Oracle Cards, they are insightful and helpful and also something physical which can connect you even more closely with the Angelic Realm. They are fun ☺

At the end of every chapter in this book, you will find an Angelic Card Exercise which will help you to get even more out of each chapter and will and help you to develop your very own special relationship with each of the Archangels.

How Do I Use My Oracle Cards?

The first thing to do is to hold your Oracle Cards. Gently take your Oracle Cards into both hands and fill them with Love and all that Love means to you. Allow your cards to become warmed by your hands and full of your energy. Shuffle your Oracle Cards gently and take your time to enjoy the pleasure of the experience. You are demonstrating to yourself that you care for yourself through this process and you are showing the Angels your commitment to yourself and your desire for positive change.

Then, read each question in the Card Exercise section of each chapter to yourself and think of the issue you would like the Angels to help you with and draw a card.

How Do I Choose a Card?

There are many ways of choosing a card and no way is right or wrong. You may like to cut the pack of cards, you may like to fan your Oracle cards out in front of you, you may like to lay your cards out in a particular shape or form. Whichever way you choose, do so calmly and lovingly.

Anticipate clarity and Love and accuracy from your Oracle Cards, expect them to help you and they will.

Jumping Cards and Falling Cards

Sometimes cards 'jump' or 'fall' out of the pack when you are shuffling them. This is the Angels giving you a card which you need to see. It may be a card which is in answer to the question to you are asking. Very often it is a card which contains a message they would like you to hear in relation to another issue in your life. Just take a moment and a breath to see what you are being shown.

Which Oracle Cards Should I Use?

The answer is any oracle cards which you like and enjoy using. You may have a favourite pack of Oracle Cards at home or a selection to choose from, just use the Oracle Cards you like. If you love them, they will love you back.

Should I Use 'Archangel' Oracle Cards?

For the purpose of this book, I would recommend that you use Archangel Cards as they will help you to establish a clear connection with the Archangels.

Angelic Visualisations

In each chapter of this book you will find an Angelic Visualisation. Each Angelic Visualisation was given to me by the Archangels to share with you, so that you can work more closely with them. The Angelic Visualisations are loving and powerful and will really help you to become more connected to the Archangels.

Each Angelic Visualisation will help you to become more familiar with the Archangels and will focus on a specific area of your life. I would encourage you to use and enjoy the many benefits they will bring into your life.

How to Use Your Archangel Visualisations

The Angelic Visualisations in this book have been abbreviated for you, so that you can follow the steps by returning to the book for each stage if you wish. There are lots of ways of enjoying them and I would encourage you to be creative. You can read the visualisations as you would the rest of the book, or you could read them out loud, you could record your own voice or you could ask a friend or loved one to read the visualisations out for you at a planned special Angel time together.

All 8 of the Angelic Visualisations from this book are available for you at my website, *www.angels-with-ros.com/book1*

Each Angelic Visualisation recording will bring you even closer to the Archangels and enhance your Angelic connection for years and years to come.

Whichever way you choose, enjoy your Angelic Visualisations for the improvement and enhancement they bring into your life.

Allow yourself some quiet and peaceful time with the Archangels in your visualisations and I promise you, you will be glad that you did.

Chapter One

The Angelic Realm

Chapter One

The Angelic Realm

By the end of this chapter you will:

- ♥ Understand more about the Angelic Realm

- ♥ Understand Angelic Hierarchy

- ♥ Have set your intention for your experience of *'Lightworking with Angels'*

- ♥ Have received the Archangels' further guidance and advice with Oracle Cards

Who Are the Angels?

Angels are infinitely powerful Lightbeings. They are not limited by distance or time, and are able to be with everybody simultaneously and enjoy a unique experience with each of us. Angels are free from all earthly limitations such as ego, personality and opinion, and because of this, they will never judge you, doubt you or criticise your choices or actions. You will never be out of favour with the Angels, they never see your faults and they will never tire of helping you to improve your life. The Angels will always, always love you, without exception and without condition.

Angels are non-physical beings existing at the high frequency of unconditional Love. They are non denominational and as such, they are here to help all of us, no matter what our beliefs or perspective. There are references to Angels in many religious texts. Christianity, Judaism and Islam all have strong and positive references to the Angels, and I have always felt this demonstrates their desire throughout history to unify and bring peace to Humankind.

What Is the Universe?

The Universe is everything that is. Everything you know, can imagine, have thought or will feel forms part of the Universe, and *everything* that happens, is said, thought, created or imagined, contributes to its continuous expansion. The Universe will never stop expanding. You are an essential part of the Universe; you are of enormous value and your life counts in many, hundreds and thousands of ways.

Your individual contribution to the expansion of the Universe is more significant than you will ever allow yourself credit for, and it is what makes you uniquely cherished and treasured. You are very, very valued indeed, and your ability to understand the way in which our eternally loving and benevolent Universe works will allow you to move through life with greater ease and enjoyment. It will help you to make sense of life's mysteries and give you back your full creative knowledge and power.

The Universe follows a strict cosmic order within its constant expansion and never-ending evolution. In order to preserve constant Universal harmony, a structured hierarchy has always existed which is formed of many important energies and light beings. The Angels form one of the many groups of light energy within the many planes of existence, dimensions of time and consciousness which construct the Universe. The Angels exist in the highest dimensions of pure Love known as the Angelic Realm.

The Angelic Realm

The Angelic Realm is a dimension of pure Love and infinite power. The Angels of the Angelic Realm exist in a dimension without lateral time, without judgment, without ego, and without any other earthly constraint.

In the Angelic Realm, time does not exist as we know it here on Earth. The Angels cannot 'run out' of time or 'be late' – it is not possible. The Angels can indeed *travel* in our time and bring healing and Love into your past, present *and* future.

The Angels would like me to explain that each Angel has the ability to be with every single person in the world at exactly the same time, sharing a completely unique experience.

The Angels would like you to know that when you ask them to be with you, they will come to you immediately, every time, without question – for all eternity. You will never take them from 'more important' or' more deserving' people or situations.

The concept of one person being more worthy or more justified or more important or more in need, does not exist. And they ask me to tell you again that the Angels have the ability to be with every single person in the world at exactly the same time, sharing a completely unique experience, and helping all equally..

Your call to the Angels is just as worthy and important as anyone else's.

The Angels would like you to know that, the Love of the Angelic Realm is limitless, eternal and available to you at all times. All you need to do is ask.

When you ask the Angels for their help, you open your heart to receive their unconditional Love and allow them to help you. When you ask the Angels for their help, you will open up to receive their Love which will transform every area of your life, and empower you with a creative force you have forgotten.

All you need to do is ask.

Focusing on What You Want

We are here as humans on Earth, we are physical in a physical plane of existence and we are an essential part of the Universe. The Angels tell me that each and every individual on Earth has a part to play in the never ending process of Creation.

Your thoughts, feelings, words and actions are all heard and understood by the Angelic Realm as 'vibrations' of energy. The Angels call these vibrations your 'Universal Voice' and they are the way that every being and energy in the Universe communicates. Your 'vibration' or Universal Voice is heard by the Universe and responded to immediately, every time, without exception and it is the means through which you manifest. The Universe and the Angels always say 'Yes' to us. But what are you *saying* with your Universal Voice? What are you asking for?

We must learn to allow the Angels' response to our requests to reach us. We must also learn to ask for what it is we actually want. By this, the Angels tell me that focusing on what you are fed up with, or irritated by, or angry about, or feeling the lack of, or wishing would go away, is not asking for what you want, it's drawing to you more of what you already have.

The Universe is inclusive and as such 'not' wanting does not exist. This is because when you are feeling 'not' wanting something, you are still asking for it. Your Universal Voice is a positive and powerful creative instrument which when used consciously will bring you everything you have ever wanted and so much more.

Understanding how the Universe and the Angelic Realm work will give you a firm foundation upon which to build your understanding of the Archangels, and really tap in to their incredible ability to help you in every way.

The Orders of Angels and Archangels

The Angels and Archangels of the Angelic Realm observe clearly defined 'Orders' in the form of an Angelic Hierarchy. Each Order has its own very clear and defined area of Universal responsibility and authority, and each Angel has an individual purpose. Each and every Angel transmits an eternal message of Love throughout their work, the vibration of which can be received and felt by us here on Earth, if we allow it.

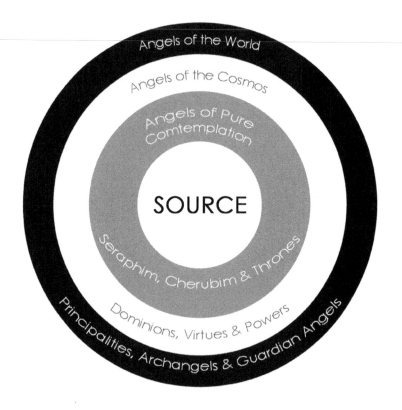

Imagine a series of ever increasing concentric circles with Source energy at the centre. This is how the Angelic Realm looks. Source is a limitless source of Love energy with many names such as the Divine, the Universe, the Creator, God and All that Is - you may like to choose a name that resonates with you. It is important to feel comfortable with the name you use to describe the centre of pure Love in the very middle of the Universe. For the purpose of this book, I will talk about 'Source'.

The beautiful, infinite, pure, positive Love energy of Source is the most powerful energy in the whole Universe – it is quite literally the 'source' of the Universe and can be found at its very centre.

You are always connected to Source whether you realise it or not. There is an energetic connection between you and Source which joins you forever. The Angels have shown me that your connection with Source is a golden stream of light which connects you on every level. You may have forgotten on a conscious level, but the Angels wish to convey to you that *you* are loved unconditionally and infinitely by Source for everything you are, everything you have ever been and everything you are going to be. *You are so loved.*

From Source at its centre, the Angelic Realm extends outwards in three Angelic circles or bands. These bands contain the three Orders of Angels and denote Angelic hierarchy, the Order closest to Source being the First Order, followed by the Second Order and then the Third Order of Angels.

All of the Angels exist within these three separate Angelic Orders, and each observes their own Angelic hierarchy within their own Order.

Each Angelic Order has its own area of Universal responsibility and each Angel within that Order has their own Divine Purpose. It is this Divine Purpose which created each Angel's individual specialism and the message that they are charged with spreading throughout the Universe.

Every Angel's message is Love – the most powerful energy in the Universe and from the message of Love, each Angel's Divine Purpose is radiated. The Love of Angels can transform you and your life beyond anything you can imagine from where you are now...

The First Order of Angels

The Angels of Pure Contemplation

The Angels of Pure Contemplation form the First Order of Angels and are the first hierarchy. The Angels of Pure Contemplation and are the Angels closest to Source and these magnificent light beings are the Seraphim, the Cherubim and the Thrones. These Angels are the highest ranking of all Angelic beings and have direct access to Source. The Angels of Pure Contemplation are responsible for communicating pure Love to all parts of the Universe and rarely take 'action' as we would think of it. These Angels contemplate, meditate and radiate.

The Angels of Contemplation are shrouded in mystery and wonder and do not have direct contact with us here on Earth.

The Seraphim

The Seraphim (singularly Seraph) are the six winged Angels who have direct communication with Source. As such, the Seraphim have the ability and responsibility to communicate pure Divine knowledge to the Universe.

The Cherubim

The Cherubim are second only to the Seraphim in the Angelic hierarchy. These powerful, four winged, light beings, join the Seraphim to spread divine knowledge throughout the entire Universe.

The Thrones

The Thrones, sometimes known as the Wheels, complete the first Order of Angels. All Angels from lower hierarchies need the Thrones to access Source and the Thrones are the only Angels of the first Order to take any form of action as well as 'contemplate'.

The Second Order of Angels

The Angels of the Cosmos

The Angels of the Cosmos form the second Order of Angels and the middle section of the Angelic Realm. Within the Second Order of Angels, there are three groups of Angels, their proximity to Source denoting their ranking within their Order. These are the Dominions, the Virtues and the

Powers. Each has occasional direct interactions with Humankind in certain special circumstances.

The Dominions

The Dominions regulate the duties of all the Angels of their own Order and also the responsibilities of the Third Orders of Angels. As such, the Dominions oversee all actions and individual Angelic responsibility, and help to conserve the structure of the Order and hierarchies within.

The Virtues

The Virtues are associated with acts of great personal sacrifice and heroism. There are many, many times throughout history when individuals have demonstrated complete self-sacrifice and bravery; The Virtues were always present. The Virtues inspire compassion and peace through their presence.

The Powers

The Powers' responsibility is to preserve balance within the Universe. The Powers help to radiate an understanding of the Laws of the Universe. The Archangels may interact with the Powers on occasion in order to bring new Universal understandings when we are ready for them here on Earth.

The Third Order of Angels

The Angels of the World

The Angels of the World are the Third Order of the Angelic Realm and work closely with us here on Planet Earth. The three hierarchies within this final Order are - The Principalities, the Archangels and the Guardian Angels.

The Principalities

The Principalities protect faith among us; they give Love to our hope and assist us in our ability to trust in a benevolent Universe. The Principalities work with Humankind to assist our ascension towards the higher realms where we can access the purest energies and light. It is the Principalities who transmit to us our ability to trust in Love.

The Archangels

The Archangels carry the wisdom of Source to Humankind. Part of the Archangels' work is to help shift Earth's consciousness towards a higher vibration of Love, compassion and humility. The Archangels will work with each of us individually to help us to fulfill our unique life's purpose. As our individual levels of Love and appreciation are increased we contribute to the upwards shift of humankind's consciousness collectively. Your life matters. Your life counts and you really *do* make a difference.

The Archangels will help you to make any change, overcome any block, and resolve any problem or issue in your life. There is no problem too big or too small for the Archangels, and they will help you in your life as much as you allow them to. Archangels always respect your free will as a human and will never interfere in any issue if their help is not requested.

The Guardian Angels

Your Guardian Angel was present and your birth into the physical world and will remain by your side for your entire lifetime. Your Guardian Angel is your own Angel of True Life Purpose and exists only for you. Your Guardian Angel is with you right now as you read these words. Many of us have felt the presence of our Guardian Angels at difficult times in our lives and many of us have been aware of our Guardian Angel stepping into dangerous situations to save us. They will keep you safe from harm and ensure that your life does not end before it is your time to pass.

Each Guardian Angel has a unique name, a special number and embodies each of our unique life purpose strengths. The Guardian Angels exist in order to keep their promise to guide us safely to our true purpose in life.

An Angelic Exercise for You to Enjoy

Intention

It is time now for you to set your intention for this book.

The Law of Intention is one of the many powerful Laws of the Universe. Intention is a clear thought and commitment to an outcome which you have decided upon. Intention can be thought of as a powerful arrow, with a completely clear flight path which is destined for a definite target in your life.

It is time now for you to set your intention for your experience of *'Lightworking with Angels'*. What would you like this book to do for you? What changes would you like to see? What would you like to experience? What outcomes which you like the Angels to bring to you? How would you like to feel having completed this book? What is it you would like to achieve?

So, close your eyes and visualise yourself having read this book. What would you like to see? Once you have decided, write your intentions down and then give it to the Angels to deliver to you at the end of this course.

My intentions through reading *'Lightworking with Angels'* are:

_____

_____

_____

_____

_____

_____

Now call upon the Angels by saying:

"Angels of the World, I am sending you my intentions and I ask that you return them to me in their highest form and in the perfect way. I send my intentions to you with Love and appreciation. And so it is."

Chapter I – Visualisation

The Angelic Realm

Moving Closer to the Angelic Realm

The purpose of this visualisation is to become closer to the Angelic Realm by giving yourself permission to accept the Love of Angels. You will learn how to open your heart to the pure Love that exists in the Angelic Realms and bring the qualities of Love and Compassion to yourself, your life and your loved ones.

You will strengthen your connection with the Angelic Realm and you will begin to recognise Angelic energy in a way which will blossom and develop beautifully over time.

1. Sit quietly with your eyes closed and relax your body. Place your hands gently in your lap with your palms facing upwards. Imagine your whole body relaxing and becoming physically comfortable.

2. Give this Angelic experience to yourself as a gift; an unconditional gift. A gift which allows you to develop yourself, to move closer to the Angelic Realm.

3. Become aware of your breath and allow your focus to gently turn to rest with your own rhythm and notice how comfortable it is. Allow yourself to enjoy full inhalations of breath and feel your heart reaching upwards to the Angels as you do.

4. Think of yourself as a colour now. Choose a colour which is the colour of Love to you. Choose a colour which you want to Be and feel. Choose a colour which feels good to your heart and enriches your soul. Whichever colour you choose will be perfect.

5. Imagine that this beautiful colour of Love fills every part of your body. Imagine it becoming you and your energy.

6. Imagine your coloured energy, expanding outwards now with the desire to connect with the Angels. The Angels have seen your coloured light and feel your desire to experience their loving presence in your life. You are moving closer to the Angels than ever before.

7. Imagine your heart opening like a beautiful flower now and accept the Love of the Angelic Realm. Give your heart the permission it needs to accept Love. Give your heart the permission it needs to accept the Love of the Angelic Realm.

8. Feel the increased ability that you have to accept the Love of the Angelic Realm. Notice how much closer you feel to the Angels. Choose to accept more Angelic Love now and be enriched and nourished by it and feel yourself becoming more loved and more loving. Allow yourself on all levels, to receive the Love and compassion from the Angelic Realm.

9. Spend some time now to become familiar with the Angelic energy that surrounds you. Enjoy the pure and loving sensations that you are experiencing. Take time now to see or feel or become aware of, any impressions of the Angelic Realm and know that these impressions will become stronger over time.

10. Thank the Angels for helping you to move closer to the Angelic Realm and acknowledge your beautiful experience today.

An Angelic Card Exercise for You to Enjoy

Take a moment to read about Oracle Card Reading on page 7 before you begin.

As you have seen in Chapter 1, The Archangels will help you to make any change, overcome any block, and resolve any problem or issue in your life. There is no problem too big or too small for the Archangels, and they will help you in your life as much as you allow them to.

Take your Oracle Cards in your hands and fill them with Love and all that Love means to you. Allow your cards to become warmed by your hands. Gently shuffle your cards and take your time and enjoy your connection with them. Anticipate clarity and Love from your cards; expect them to help you and they will.

When you are ready, ask the Archangels:

'Loving Archangels, please provide me with your loving guidance'

Now choose a card for each of the questions below.

Note down the cards as you choose them and what you feel that they are conveying to you.

1. What is it that the Archangels would like to communicate to me today?

2. How can I learn more about my purpose here on Earth?

3. How can I become more open to connecting with the Archangels?

4. What can I develop within myself today in order to work with the Archangels more powerfully?

And when you have finished, thank the Archangels for their help by simply saying 'Thank you'.

The Angelic Realm

My Thoughts, Feelings and Requests

This is the very special place for you to record your thoughts and feelings. Use this very special place to ask the Angels to help you with anything which you become aware of or would like to ask for, as you move through the chapters of this book.

Chapter Two

Introducing the Archangels

Chapter Two

Introducing the Archangels

By the end of this chapter you will:

- ❤ Have called the Archangels to be with you with an Angelic Invocation

- ❤ Understand how the Archangels can help you to improve your life

- ❤ Have strengthened your connection with the Archangels

- ❤ Have received the Archangels' further guidance and advice with Oracle Cards

Archangel Invocation

Take a moment to read about invocations on page 5 before you begin.

It's time to connect with the Angelic Realm now and to call the Archangels to be with you. So, close your eyes and give yourself permission for this experience.

Now, take some relaxing breaths and gently focus your intention and full expectation upon connecting with the Archangels. It is your intention and expectation to connect with them which will allow your channel of Angelic communication to become open.

And now ask the Archangels to be with you.

The Archangels are with you right now.

Open your heart to their safe, secure and loving aura.

Feel with all of your senses and see in your mind's eye, the rainbow colours of the Archangels.

Ask them to surround you with their Love energy and ask them to direct it to the parts of you which need it right now. Do that now.

Now spend some time, becoming more familiar with the Archangels' energy.

Ask the Archangels to help you to recognise their energy every time they are near you.

Ask that the Archangels stay with you throughout this chapter.

And so it is.

Introducing the Archangels

In this chapter I'd like to introduce you to Archangels Michael, Gabriel, Raphael, Chamuel, Zadkiel and Metatron. Each is limitlessly powerful, and each of them has their own area of Angelic specialism and Divine Purpose. Knowing what these specialisms are will help you to get to know the Archangels and achieve a strong and meaningful connection with each them. It is through your familiarity and personal relationship with the Archangels, that you will come to understand how they can help you in your life.

The Archangels have a unique relationship with everyone, and they can communicate with you through your senses in different ways depending on how best you receive information. You may be a visual person, or Clairvoyant; you may be somebody who hears information, otherwise known as a Clairaudient; you may *feel* guidance and be a Clairsentient; or you may just *know* what is being conveyed to you - this way of receiving the wisdom of the Angels is known as Claircognizance.

All of these ways of connecting with the Archangels should be valued and appreciated for the relationship to the Angelic Realm they create. Honour and value your particular communication channel with all of the Angels, and know that it is perfect for you.

Your connection with the Archangels may begin very subtly at first, with only a gentle awareness that they are with you. You may not know which Archangel is with you for some time, but you will begin to recognize their very unique energies with practice and the desire to do so.

The Archangels are gentle and patient. They will keep on helping you and they will give you all the time you need to develop your gift at a speed with which you are comfortable.

Enjoy developing your relationship with the Archangels and accept it, no matter how far away it is from how you want it to be. Acknowledge any sensations and feelings no matter how small or subtle you consider them to be. Your ability will be strengthened over time and the extent to which you can accept and embrace any level of connection with the Archangel will see it grow. Your

intention to connect with the Archangels of the
Angelic Realm will see it become reality.

Archangel Michael

Archangel Michael – Leader of the Archangels

Aura – Deep Blue Indigo

Crystal – Lapis Lazuli

Chakras – Root, Third Eye

Embodies – Courage, Strength, Truth

Primary Role – Freedom from Negative Energy

Areas of Your Life – Relationships, Personal & Spiritual Development

Archangel Michael is the leader of the Archangels and oversees all of the work of the Angels of the Archangels and the Guardian Angels. He is the Archangel of courage, strength and truth, and is often pictured as a beautiful, strong and powerful male. Archangel Michael carries a sword of truth and a shield of protection, and his energy embodies infinite courage and power.

Michael has a deep blue aura which is so strong it feels almost solid, yet it is also incredibly tender and loving. Michael's aura radiates a vast, masculine energy which feels completely safe and secure. It's like warm, loving arms all around you, reassuring and soothing every part of your being. He reminds you that 'All is well', and helps you to accept that you are completely and unconditionally loved.

Michael is an Angel who carries a lot of heat in his energy. The room often becomes incredibly warm whenever he's around, and this is one of the ways he can help you to know that he is present.

Archangel Michael's primary role is to free you from any negative energy in your life and realign you with the energy of positivity and Love. He will help you to reconnect with your true self, and to understand the freedom that comes from living your life from a place of Love.

Archangel Michael can free you from any negative issues which remain with you from your past. These issues often stay stuck in your life, and may result in an inability to move on from a difficult relationship or a traumatic event from your past.

An inability to move on from people in your past is often created by an etheric cord. Michael can release you from the past by disconnecting you from the etheric cords which hold you there. He will sever the ties that keep you stuck in a painful place, that drain your spiritual and physical energy levels and prevent you from moving on with your life. We will talk lots more about etheric cords later in Chapter 3.

Michael will encourage and support you to be 'All that You Are', and help you to regain your lost confidence. He is there to support you when you doubt yourself, and is the deep breath you take as you move into new areas of your life. Michael will encourage and support you out of your 'comfort zone'. A place which is very often far from comfortable - just familiar and predictable!

Archangel Michael will also help you to move through life in a way that is fulfilling and uplifting and directed towards discovering your Life Purpose.

I have seen unimaginable transformation in people's lives through working with Archangel

Michael - we will learn more about him in Chapter 3.

Archangel Tips:

- ♥ *Michael can be called upon to surround you and your loved ones with his cloak of safety and security*

- ♥ *Michael can free you from your past by cutting through etheric cords*

- ♥ *Michael will encourage you and support you to become 'All That You Are'*

- ♥ *Michael will help you to develop spiritually*

Archangel Gabriel

Archangel Gabriel – Angel of Communication

Aura – Sparkling Golden and White

Crystal – Yellow Calcite

Chakra – Throat

Embodies – Empowerment, Honesty

Primary Role – To Empower You to Reach Your Highest Potential

Areas of Your Life – Career, Self-Belief & Communication

Archangel Gabriel is the Archangel of Communication, sometimes referred to as the Messenger Angel. Archangel Gabriel has a beautiful golden, sparkling aura and often appears as a feminine energy.

Archangel Gabriel will help you to express yourself truthfully and to communicate effectively and honestly with the world. She can help you to be clear with friends, family and colleagues, and she reminds you that you cannot communicate honestly and effectively with others unless you are honest with yourself. It is important to be honest about your needs and desires, and to become aware of the freedom that such honesty will bring you.

Archangel Gabriel will also help you to communicate effectively with all of the other Archangels. She will help you to develop and strengthen all of your intuitive ability and spiritual gifts. Gabriel is the Archangel to call upon if you would like to develop and strengthen your existing communication channels with the Angels. She will also help you to open new spiritual channels for receiving the Archangels' guidance.

Archangel Gabriel is also an incredible angelic asset to enhance your career. If you would like to optimise where you are in your career or develop a new more successful and fulfilling career, she will help you to see possibilities and opportunities.

Gabriel will give you the confidence to follow your inner truth; she will fill you with more self belief, and help you to break through any limitations from your past. Gabriel will help you to identify your true needs and ask the Universe for them.

Allow Archangel Gabriel to help you live your life in your power, to fulfil your dreams and to turn your ideas into reality. She is a hugely empowering and enabling Archangel who will help you to feel the sense of self-worth and personal value which is your birthright.

Archangel Tips:

- ♥ *Gabriel can be called upon to help you find anything which is 'lost' or has been misplaced*

- ♥ *Gabriel will help you to speak your truth*

- ♥ *Gabriel can be called upon when making any decisions which relate to your career*

Archangel Raphael

Archangel Raphael – The Healing Angel

Aura – Emerald Green

Crystal – Green Aventurine

Chakra – Heart

Embodies – Healing, Wellbeing

Primary Role - To Help You to Experience the Flow of Wellbeing in Every Part of Your Life

Areas of Your Life – Emotional, Spiritual & Physical Wellbeing

Archangel Raphael has a bright emerald green aura and radiates a powerful healing light to all those who call upon him. Known as the Healing Angel, Raphael can heal any emotional, physical or spiritual pain and in addition to helping you, he will also help you to develop your ability to heal others.

Archangel Raphael tells us that freedom from physical pain can be achieved when we release the emotional issues to which the illness, disease or discomfort are anchored. He says that every physical imbalance is a manifestation of an emotional misalignment within ourselves. He tells us that when we close our hearts, we are preventing ourselves from being healed by the flow of wellbeing that an open heart allows. Archangel Raphael tells us that forgiveness and compassion are the first stages to our healing. We can all be healed; Raphael can help us to live in the state of wellbeing that is our birthright.

Throughout history, Lightworkers have been persecuted and punished for their beliefs and gifts. The fear and pain experienced by our ancestors, and in our previous lives, can follow us through many generations and incarnations. Archangel Raphael can help us to heal the wounds of the past and bring healing into future generations.

Raphael helps us to remember the freedom of unconditional forgiveness. Forgiveness is freedom from pain. Forgiveness puts an end to everything that has gone before. Forgiveness frees you and frees your future. Raphael tells us that forgiveness and healing are intertwined, and that he can fill us with the strength we need to face our deepest fears and darkest moments.

Archangel Raphael can be called upon to bring healing to difficult or challenging relationships, providing balance and Love to all those concerned. He will help you all to find a place where wellbeing can reach all parties and wounds can heal without scars. He will help you open your heart to love and help you to experience true happiness and contentment in your life. He will show you how to offer the Love you have deep inside your heart, so that you in turn can receive that same Love from others.

Archangel Raphael can help you become a channel for his healing power, to facilitate healing for yourself or others. He tells you that the part you play in another's healing is far more significant than you imagine. Every time you think of another, you send them energy and this energy can be positive and beneficial and health giving. Raphael explains that when a loved one is in need of healing, you benefit them greatly by sending them positive energy with your thoughts. Send them wellbeing, health, vitality and physical nourishment. Think of them as you would like to find them.

Raphael will help you to develop your ability to heal on all levels and in every way.

Archangel Tips:

- ❤ *Raphael can help you to develop your healing ability*

- ❤ *Raphael can be called upon to surround your loved ones with his emerald green healing aura*

- ❤ *Raphael can be called upon whenever you wish to feel more energized or vital*

Archangel Chamuel

Archangel Chamuel – The Angel of Love

Aura – Soft Pink

Crystal – Rose Quartz

Chakra – Sacral

Embodies – Unconditional Love

Primary Role - To Help Us to Become More Loved and Loving

Areas of Your Life – Self Love, Relationships & Attracting Positivity

Archangel Chamuel is the Archangel of Unconditional Love who encourages you to love yourself more and to appreciate and value all that you are. Archangel Chamuel has a beautiful pink, sparkling aura, and a gentle and comforting energy. Archangel Chamuel will help you to see yourself as the Angels see you - as a vision of pure Love and beauty.

The Angels tell me that they see us as a vision of everyone we have ever loved or been loved by, every time we've ever trusted and been open and loving, every time we've ever smiled or laughed, and as every drop of happiness that we have ever experienced in our lives. Try seeing that next time you look in the mirror.

Archangel Chamuel's presence is wonderful for healing damaged relationships. Chamuel will bring a positive resolution to a misunderstanding or difference of opinion, and help all those involved to move on with their lives.

Archangel Chamuel will help you to open your heart so that you radiate the quality of Love that you yourself wish to experience in your relationships. He will help you to see the loving qualities in others, bring lovers closer together, and unify families through difficult times.

Archangel Chamuel will help you to find new and positive people to enrich your life, such as like-minded friends and colleagues who share your interests. He can help you to find your soulmate and experience a deep and loving relationship, and can help you to raise your vibration and your self-esteem, so that you attract Love in all its forms.

Archangel Tips:

- ❤ *Chamuel can help you to find your soulmate*

- ❤ *Chamuel can help you to open your heart*

- ❤ *Chamuel can be called upon to bring more Love and laughter to families*

Archangel Zadkiel

Archangel Zadkiel – The Angel of Transformation

Aura – Lilac and Golden

Crystal – Amethyst

Chakra – Solar Plexus

Embodies – Abundance and Joy

Primary Role - To Release Unforgiveness

Areas of Your Life – Manifestation & Change

Archangel Zadkiel is the Archangel of Transformation who works with the powerful Violet Flame of Transmutation. He is known as the 'Bringer of Joy', and will help you to manifest abundance into all areas of your life. Zadkiel radiates a powerful violet aura which is flecked with the golden light of positivity, and has the power to release you from old patterns of behaviour which might be limiting your experience of life.

Zadkiel tells us that it is the negativity in our lives which stops us receiving everything we want. He offers to take away our negativity and exchange it for Love in all its forms.

Archangel Zadkiel's primary role is to help you to let go of any unforgiveness that you hold in your heart. He asks that you call upon him when you are ready to forgive yourself and others for any pain or sadness in your life. Zadkiel can help you to understand that forgiveness is an incredible healing force that enables you to discover your true, loving nature. Forgiveness doesn't apportion blame or mean something wasn't painful to you, it means that you are ready to be free from the emotion of the experience.

Zadkiel represents the willingness to let go of any resistance to receiving, not only through forgiveness, but through the generosity of an open and loving heart. By releasing your heavy feelings, Zadkiel can provide you with a direct connection to the limitless abundance of Source and the Universe.

Archangel Zadkiel can help you to release *any* negative feelings or thoughts that you have about yourself or someone else, from anger to self loathing. He can help you to release any negative behaviour patterns which prevent you from moving forward with your life, and by doing so, experience the joy and gifts of the Universe which you came to Earth to enjoy.

Archangel Tips:

- ♥ *Zadkiel can free you from patterns of self criticism and blame*

- ♥ *Zadkiel can renew your faith in the abundance of the Universe*

- ♥ *Zadkiel can help you to see how your life could be without the negative thoughts and feelings which do not serve or benefit you*

Archangel Metatron

Archangel Metatron – Angel of Inspiration, Motivation and Miracles

Aura – Silver, Golden, Violet

Crystal – Clear Quartz

Chakra – Crown

Embodies – Balance, Miracles, Motivation

Primary Role - To Help Us to Take Positive Action in our Lives

Areas of Your Life – Expressing Your Higher Self, Living Your Life Purpose, Children

Archangel Metatron is known as the Angel of Inspiration, Motivation and Miracles and as such embodies positive action and proactivity. Metatron radiates an incredible aura of silver, golden and violet and often works closely with Archangel Michael on great creative tasks throughout the Universe. Archangel Metatron is the Angel to call upon if you need help to complete a task, have trouble taking action, feel overwhelmed or need an injection of inspiration.

Archangel Metatron is the Archangel who will whisper to you the words of inspiration you need to motivate yourself into taking positive action in your life. He will help you to conquer seemingly overwhelming tasks and learn valuable Spiritual lessons along the way. Miracles are likely to happen when Archangel Metatron is around.

If you need help to get yourself going again, or you need to draw upon some enthusiasm from somewhere to energise your life, Archangel Metatron will help you. Metatron is the Archangel to call upon of you need help you to get a task completed, get your paperwork finished or organised, tie up a long outstanding matter or just get some forwards movement and action going again in your life.

Archangel Metatron works closely with all those who support and empower children, and can be called upon to help children to develop their Spiritual gifts. He is often referred to as the 'Leader of all Children', and helps every child and young person, both on Earth and in Heaven, to achieve great works.

Archangel Metatron will help you to develop your Spiritual self and your ability to listen to your Soul's voice. He can be called upon to help you to discover and develop your Life Purpose, and to achieve a harmonious balance between your personal and spiritual self.

Archangel Tips:

- ♥ *Metatron can help you to take action if you tend to procrastinate*

- ♥ *Metatron can help you if you feel overwhelmed*

- ♥ *Metatron can help you to develop a positive career with Children and Young People*

Chapter 2 – Visualisation

Introducing the Archangels

Introducing the Energy of the Archangels

The purpose of this visualisation is to strengthen your relationship with Archangels Michael, Gabriel and Raphael Chamuel, Zadkiel and Metatron. You will call each Archangel to be with you in turn and discover how the energy of each Angel feels to you.

1. Sit quietly with your eyes closed and relax your body. Place your hands gently in your lap with your palms facing upwards. Imagine your whole body relaxing and becoming physically comfortable.

2. Give this Angelic experience to yourself as a gift; an unconditional gift. A gift which allows you to develop yourself, to move closer to the Angelic Realm.

3. Become aware of your breath and allow your focus to gently turn to rest with your own rhythm and notice how comfortable it is. Allow yourself to enjoy full inhalations of breath and feel your heart reaching upwards to the Angels as you do.

4. Imagine that the Archangels are sending to you a warm and soothing wave of relaxing, loving energy. Welcome that energy and let it reach every part of you. Imagine your arms are open wide to embrace the loving and peaceful energy which the Archangels send to you.

5. Call Archangel Michael, Leader of the Archangels, to be with you now and know that your call to him has been responded to immediately. Imagine Archangel Michael's deep blue aura surrounding your whole body, filling you with a deep sense of security and complete reassurance. Imagine Michael is now sending you the qualities of strength and courage.

6. Call upon Archangel Gabriel, Angel of Empowerment, to be with you and know that your call to her has been responded to immediately. Imagine Archangel Gabriel's golden and white, sparkling aura surrounding you and filling you with a deep sense of empowerment and truth. Imagine Gabriel is now sending you the qualities of empowerment and truth.

7. Call Archangel Raphael, the Healing Angel, be with you and know that your call to him has been responded to immediately. Imagine Archangel Raphael's beautiful, emerald green aura surrounding you and filling you with his healing energy. Imagine Raphael is now sending you a heavenly stream of Well-being.

8. Call upon Archangel Chamuel, the Angel of Love, to be with you and know that your call to him has been responded to immediately. Imagine Archangel Chamuel's tender pink aura surrounding you and filling you with his loving energy. Imagine Chamuel is now sending you an increased ability to accept the qualities of Love.

9. Call Archangel Zadkiel, the Angel of Transformation, to be with you and know that your call to him has been responded to immediately. Imagine Archangel Zadkiel's purple and violet aura surrounding you and filling you with his positive energy. Imagine Archangel Archangel Zadkiel is helping you to make space in your heart for abundance and the life of your dreams.

10. Call upon Archangel Metatron, the Angel of Miracles, and know that your call to him has been responded to immediately. Imagine Archangel Metatron's silver, golden and violet aura surrounding you and filling you with his miraculous and motivational energy. Imagine Metatron sending you the inspiration you need to take positive action in your life.

11. Thank all of the Archangels for their presence and send appreciation for the Angelic energy and qualities that they have brought into your life today.

An Angelic Card Exercise for You to Enjoy

Take a moment to read about Oracle Card Reading on page 7 before you begin.

As you have seen in Chapter 2, the Archangels can help you to experience more Love in all areas of your life. The Archangels can help you to welcome improvement and move onwards and upwards to better and better things. It is now time to ask the Archangels to provide you with their guidance and further insight through Oracle Cards.

Take your Oracle Cards in your hands and fill them with Love and all that Love means to you. Allow your cards to become warmed by your hands. Gently shuffle your cards and take your time and enjoy your connection with them. Anticipate clarity and Love from your cards; expect them to help you and they will.

When you are ready, ask the Archangels:

'Loving Archangels, please provide me with your loving guidance'

Now choose a card for each of the questions below.

Note down the cards as you choose them and what you feel that they are conveying to you.

1. What is it the Archangels would like me to know as I begin my journey with them?

2. Which quality can I develop within myself in order to become closer to the Archangels?

3. Which part of my life are the Archangels helping me to understand today?

4. How can I bring the Archangels even more into my everyday life?

And when you have finished, thank the Archangels for their help by simply saying 'Thank you'.

Introducing the Archangels

My Thoughts, Feelings and Requests

This is the very special place for you to record your thoughts and feelings. Use this very special place to ask the Angels to help you with anything which you become aware of or would like to ask for, as you move through the chapters of this book.

Chapter Three

Archangel Michael

Chapter Three

Archangel Michael

By the end of this chapter you will:

- ♥ Have called Archangel Michael to be with you with an Angelic Invocation

- ♥ Understand how Archangel Michael can help you to improve your life

- ♥ Have experienced the freedom of severing Etheric Cords

- ♥ Have received Archangel Michael's further guidance and advice with Oracle Cards

Archangel Michael Invocation

Take a moment to read about invocations on page 5 before you begin.

It's time to connect with the Angelic Realm now and to call Archangel Michael to be with you. So, close your eyes and give yourself permission for this experience.

Now, take some relaxing breaths and gently focus your intention and full expectation upon connecting with Archangel Michael.

It is your intention and expectation to connect with the Leader of the Archangels which will allow your channel of Angelic communication to become open.

And now ask Archangel Michael to be with you.

Archangel Michael is with you right now.

Open your heart to his safe, secure and loving aura.

Feel with all of your senses and see in your mind's eye, the deep blueness of Archangel Michael.

Ask him to surround you with his strengthening energy and ask him to direct it to the parts of you which need to feel strong and courageous and powerful. Do that now.

Now spend some time, becoming more familiar with Michael's energy.

Ask Archangel Michael to help you to recognise his energy every time he is near you.

Ask that Archangel Michael stay with you throughout this Chapter.

And so it is.

Well Done! Whether this is the first time, 50th time or the millionth time you have connected with Archangel Michael, acknowledge and appreciate your experience and know that your relationship with Michael is forever.

How Will You Experience Archangel Michael's Presence?

Remember from Chapter One, that there are many different ways of communicating with the Angels and in this case with Archangel Michael. Some people will *feel* his energy and aura, others may *see* his deep blue light and form, and there are those who will *hear* Michael's guidance or be told by him that he is with them, or it may be that you just *know* he is present. Honour and value your communication channel with him and know that it is perfect for you.

Whichever way you experience Michael's energy, your awareness may be very subtle at first. You may even think that you are imagining what you are feeling. Lots of people question their initial experiences, but I encourage you to accept how good it feels, accept Michael's safe and secure energy, and ask him to show you that he is with you in many different ways – and he will.

You may begin to notice Michael's presence through a beautiful blueness entering your life. You might be drawn to a beautiful deep blue silk scarf, or begin to notice the beauty of the sky. You might find yourself wanting to bring blue into your home, and crystals like Lapis Lazuli will begin to call to you.

Whatever you experience, enjoy and accept it, no matter how small you consider it to be. Your attention to and acceptance of your growing Angelic awareness will see it develop beautifully over time. Your intention to connect with Archangel Michael will see your relationship become stronger and clearer every day.

How Can Archangel Michael Help Me?

Archangel Michael is the Leader of the Archangels and embodies the qualities of Courage, Strength and Truth. He is waiting to help you in any area of your life where you wish to experience more freedom and positivity.

Know that *all is well.*

Archangel Michael reassures us that 'all is well' when we feel challenged or overwhelmed. He encourages us to see that everything is just as it should be and that we are able to succeed in life when we release our expectation to fail.

Feel Safe and Secure

Michael will help you to feel safe and secure in all ways, and will surround you, your loved ones, your home, your possessions and everything that you hold dear, with his powerful blue cloak of protection if you ask him to. He will protect your home when you go away on holiday, can be asked to stand guard as you sleep peacefully, and can be called upon when you are alone and feeling unsafe or insecure.

Take a moment: *Take a few minutes now to ask Archangel Michael to surround you and your loved ones with his cloak of protection. Close your eyes and ask him to protect your family and your home with his deep blue cloak, and visualise everyone surrounded by his safe and secure energy. And so it is.*

Conquer Your Fears

Michael's energy will help you to become strong from your core. If you ask him to, he will fill you with the courage you need to step out of your comfort zone and into new, exciting and unchartered territory. He will hold your hand when you lack confidence and encourage you to be brave and conquer your fears. He will go at your pace, and help you build up to achieving things and making choices which might seem unimaginable where you are now.

He will help you to get *yourself* out of your way.

Release Your Negative Patterns of Behaviour

People find that their lives become lighter and more positive when they work with Archangel Michael. They find themselves able to break through negative patterns of behaviour and change their unhelpful ways of reacting to the world.

Negative behaviour patterns can include anything from compulsive eating and unsuitable romantic choices to constant low self esteem and a low expectation of life. Michael will help you to make positive choices which allow you to enjoy where you are in your life.

Enjoy More Loving Relationships

People find that they are able to experience more positive and loving relationships when they work with Archangel Michael. Relationships are able to flourish as people learn how to identify the qualities of Love within others.

Negative Energy Attachments and Etheric Cords

When we have an emotional relationship with another person, we create energetic cords which join us and our energies together. The intensity of the relationship increases the strength of these cords. Where Love flows in a relationship, both parties flourish and exchange positive energy through their shared loving thoughts and feelings for each other. These loving cords are beneficial, eternal and can never be severed.

However, *negative* energy cords can develop between people as a result of a painful break up, a betrayal, a perceived injustice, a traumatic experience or a 'falling out. These negative cords are formed when feelings of guilt, anger, blame, hatred, revenge and unforgiveness are experienced by one party and projected to the other. Once negative energy cords are in place, negativity can be exchanged throughout whole life times and create a range of difficulties and problems for those joined together in such an unhelpful way.

Negative energy cords are very common and the existence of them does not make you abnormal or a bad person. Negative energy cords can exist between husbands and wives, partners, siblings, parents, children, lovers, past lovers, friends and acquaintances and anybody else with whom you have experienced a testing relationship.

So you can see how as you move through life with all of its emotion and unresolved issues, you can accumulate lots of negative energy cords which drain your spiritual and personal energy levels and prevent you from moving on with your life.

Etheric Cords Can Appear in All Shapes and Sizes

Etheric cords are heavy dark cords or chains which drain your energy levels and exchange constant negativity between those who are joined. Etheric cords come in all different shapes, thicknesses and lengths and range from fine hair like strands to heavy chains. All etheric cords create tangled and intertwined lengths of heaviness and fear which firmly hold those joined together, in negativity.

Archangel Michael can free you from any kind of etheric cord regardless of its age, length or thickness. He will sever the negative energy attachment by cutting through it with his sword of truth. He will easily slice through the dark and heavy cord, freeing you from negative energy and shining his powerful healing light into the opening.

You will feel a sense of calm and peace reach you as positivity is brought powerfully in to replace the negativity.

Severing Etheric Cords

Severing an etheric cord does not mean 'I don't love you,' or 'You were to blame,' and it does not lead to the end of existing relationships. In fact, etheric cords often exist in relationships where there is also much that is positive between two people. Unless dealt with, etheric cords become stronger in their negativity and more of a drain on your positive energy.

Once they have been dealt with, when the negative energy cords have been severed between two people, only positive energy can flow between them.

Severing of negative energy cords can greatly enhance loving relationships as it releases you only from the negative or dysfunctional parts of the relationship. It means that you can both be free and released from the ties that held you both in a sad or negative place in time.

Once the negative energy cords have been severed, which held past lovers together in anger and resentment, miraculous contact is often received after many years of silence, allowing wounds to be healed on both sides. It is really quite the most freeing, positive and miraculous experience.

I see time and time again the transformation in people's lives, once Michael has severed negative energy cords. People's lives become more positive, more loving and more successful. Their lives open up to experience the happiness and freedom which has been absent from many years. People find the Love that they thought they would never have. People see happiness and harmony return to their families. People resolve age-old issues from their past and experience the completion and finality they had always wished for.

Chapter 3 – Visualisation

Archangel Michael

Freedom from Your Etheric Cords

If you know that there is anger, resentment, guilt, unforgiveness or any other negative emotion between you and a loved one, or any other person in your life past or present, then you can be sure that an Etheric Cord exists between you.

In this powerful visualisation, 'Freedom from your Etheric Cords', Archangel Michael will set you free from the physical, emotional and spiritual energy drain which negative energy cords create.

By asking Archangel Michael to cut the negative energy cords which join you, you will experience a flow of positive energy into a once dark and negative space. Michael will bring you beautiful healing, by dissolving the root of the cord and filling the opening with his beautiful, healing light.

Preparing to Be Free

I'd like you to take a moment now to think of a person with whom you have experienced feelings of anger, guilt, resentment, fear or any other kind of negativity. It may be someone who is still in your life or someone who you have not seen for many years. It may be someone who is in Heaven or still very much on Earth. It may be someone that you haven't thought about for a long time but comes immediately to mind.

The purpose of the visualisation is to become free from the physical, emotional and spiritual energy drain that etheric cords create. Archangel Michael will cut the negative energy cords that join you and another person and bring you beautiful healing, by dissolving the root of the cord and filling the opening with his beautiful, healing light.

Once you have chosen a person you would like to work with, begin with your visualisation:

1. Sit quietly with your eyes closed and relax your body. Place your hands gently in your lap with your palms facing upwards. Imagine your whole body relaxing and becoming physically comfortable.

2. Give this Angelic experience to yourself as a gift; an unconditional gift. A gift which allows you to develop yourself and to grow.

3. Become aware of your breath and allow your focus to gently come to rest with your own rhythm and notice how comfortable it is. Allow yourself to enjoy full inhalations of breath and feel your heart reaching upwards to the Angels as you do.

4. Call upon Archangel Michael, Leader of the Archangels, to be with you and know that your call to him is responded to immediately. Archangel Michael is with you now.

5. Imagine Michael is surrounding you with his loving, deep blue aura and a cloak of courage and confidence.

6. Bring into your awareness the person you would like Michael to free you from negativity. Imagine them in your mind's eye or gently remember them. Give Archangel Michael your permission to free you from all of the etheric cords which join you.

7. Imagine Archangel Michael cutting through your etheric cords with his sword of truth, in one clean motion. Feel yourself released from all of the heaviness, anger, shame or regret that held this person to you. Feel your distance from all of the negative emotion.

8. Imagine beautiful Angelic Light and Love reaching you as never before as Archangel Michael shines his powerful light into the openings of the severed cords; dissolving the root and deeply healing and sealing the opening.

9. Feel your courage and strength and feel your desire to be free of all that causes you pain. Feel your desire for more positivity and happiness in your life. Feel the freedom of all that you have released.

10. Thank Archangel Michael for helping you to become free of your etheric cords.

An Angelic Card Exercise for You to Enjoy

Take a moment to read about Oracle Card Reading on page 7 before you begin.

As you have seen in Chapter 3, Archangel Michael will help you to conquer your fears, be braver, more positive and encourage you to move out of your comfort zone. It is now time to ask Archangel Michael to provide you with his guidance and further insight through Oracle Cards.

Take your Oracle Cards in your hands and fill them with Love and all that Love means to you. Allow your cards to become warmed by your hands. Gently shuffle your cards and take your time and enjoy your connection with them. Anticipate clarity and Love from your cards; expect them to help you and they will.

When you are ready, ask the Archangel Michael:

'Archangel Michael, please provide me with your loving guidance'

Now choose a card for each of the questions below.

Note down the cards as you choose them and what you feel that they are conveying to you.

1. What is it that Archangel Michael would like to communicate to me today?

2. How can I have courage to move out of my comfort zone more often?

3. How can I *identify* any patterns of negative behaviour in my life?

4. How can I *release* any patterns of negative behaviour in my life?

And when you have finished, thank Archangel Michael for his help by simply saying 'Thank you'.

Archangel Michael

My Thoughts, Feelings and Requests

This is the very special place for you to record your thoughts and feelings. Use this very special place to ask the Angels to help you with anything which you become aware of or would like to ask for, as you move through the chapters of this book.

Chapter Four

Archangel Gabriel

Chapter Four

Archangel Gabriel

By the end of this chapter you will:

- ❤ Have called Archangel Gabriel to be with you with an Angelic Invocation

- ❤ Understand how Archangel Gabriel can help you to improve your life

- ❤ Have received Archangel Gabriel's help to be more honest with yourself

- ❤ Have received Archangel Gabriel's further guidance and advice with Oracle Cards.

Archangel Gabriel Invocation

Take a moment to read about invocations on page 5 before you begin.

It's time to connect with the Angelic Realm now and to call Archangel Gabriel to be with you. So, close your eyes and give yourself permission for this experience.

Now, take some relaxing breaths and gently focus your intention and full expectation upon connecting with Archangel Gabriel.

It is your intention and expectation to connect with the Archangel of Communication which will allow your channel of Angelic communication to become open.

And now ask Archangel Gabriel to be with you.

Archangel Gabriel is with you right now.

Open your heart to her safe, secure and loving aura.

Feel with all of your senses and see in your mind's eye, the sparkling, golden and white aura of Archangel Gabriel.

Ask her to surround you with her empowering energy and ask her to direct it to the parts of you which need to help to express themselves confidently and honestly.

Ask Gabriel to help you to live your life in your power. Do that now.

Allow yourself to accept more and more of Archangel Gabriel's golden energy now.

Now spend some time, becoming more familiar with Gabriel's energy.

Ask Archangel Gabriel to help you to recognise her energy every time she is near you.

Ask that Archangel Gabriel stay with you throughout this chapter.

And so it is.

Well Done! You have now begun a wonderful
relationship with Archangel Gabriel which will
remain with you throughout your whole life. Allow
yourself to acknowledge and appreciate every
experience you have with her, and trust your
connection with her will strengthen over time.

How Will You Experience Archangel Gabriel's Presence?

Remember that everyone has a unique relationship
with the Angels. You may *feel* Archangel Gabriel's
empowering energy, *see* her golden sparkling aura,
hear her clear communication or just *know* when
Gabriel is with you. Honour and value your com-

munication channel with her and know that it is perfect for you.

Your awareness may be very gentle at first, for Gabriel will want to introduce you slowly to her energy. Angelic communication is rather like the tuning dial on a radio – you often have to play around with it to find the right channel , and it can take a bit of fine tuning before you are able to hear everything clearly. Once you have 'tuned in' to the correct channel for the Angelic Realm, you will always know where to find it and can then begin to increase the volume control!

How Can Archangel Gabriel Help Me?

Archangel Gabriel is one of the highest ranking Archangels and often works closely with Archangel Michael. Known as the Messenger Angel, she is an excellent communicator and will help you strengthen your own communication skills. Gabriel also brings news and finds answers, and can be very helpful when you need to make decisions – especially in your career.

If there is a seemingly impossible issue in your life at the moment, ask Gabriel to find you the solution before you sleep. Very often, when you wake up in the morning, the information you need will come to you.

Honest Communication from a Place of Love

Gabriel will help you to open effective communication channels within your personal life, within yourself and between you and the Angelic Realm. Effective communication comes from a place of Love within you, without any expectation or conditions. You will find that as you begin to communicate with honesty and integrity, you will find it far easier to express yourself and have your needs met. Until you are honest with yourself and honest about what you really want and need from your life, your life will never offer you what you truly want.

Clarity

Gabriel encourages you to be crystal clear in your thinking and goals. Gabriel encourages you to think about how you would like your life to be. She says that though sometimes life can be challenging, and there are often things that you wish were different or better. By visualising how you would like your life to be and focusing on what it is you love, you allow change to come. Gabriel tells you that you will always find what you are looking for in life– so be clear about what you want to find. And you will find it.

It's All About You

Allow yourself to be the change you want to see. If you feel surrounded by anger, ask Gabriel to help you emanate Love and peace. If you see a shortage of money or a lack of time in your life, ask Gabriel to show you a path towards abundance and plenty. As you ask to be shown something, expect to find it. Look for what you have asked for and see how you are always provided with evidence of Archangel's Gabriel's work.

Listening To Your Needs

Gabriel encourages you to nourish your soul by allowing yourself to take time out from all of the rush and pressure and problems you feel part of and find a place to be still and quiet. *Listen* to your needs. Honour and value yourself first, then give to your family and friends all of the true Love you experience from yourself.

Resentment is a clear sign that you are *not* listening to your needs. Gabriel asks you to pay attention to feelings of resentment, which can mount up inside you, and to ask yourself what it is that you are not being honest about. What is it that you are doing that you do not want to do? Who do you feel indebted to? What do you feel obligated to do? You are choosing to feel all of these draining emotions, and if you ask, Gabriel will help you to experience the improvement and positive change which honesty brings.

Gabriel reminds you again, to focus on what it is you *want* and feel the energy it gives to you.

Gabriel will empower you to empower yourself. Her energy will help you to identify your needs, express them effectively and see them met. She will not speak your words for you or force your hand. It is for you to accept Gabriel's help and guidance and apply it to your life.

Chapter 4 – Visualisation

Archangel Gabriel

The Empowerment of Honesty

The purpose of this visualisation is to help you to empower yourself through your own honesty. When you honour yourself by being honest and truthful with yourself, happiness and fulfillment will surround you and everything you do.

Archangel Gabriel will support you through this visualisation, to be honest, express yourself honestly and be empowered by your ability to listen to your needs.

1. Sit quietly with your eyes closed and relax your body. Place your hands gently in your lap with your palms facing upwards. Imagine your whole body relaxing and becoming physically comfortable.

2. Give this Angelic experience to yourself as a gift; an unconditional gift. A gift which allows you to develop yourself and to grow.

3. Become aware of your breath and allow your focus to gently come to rest with your own rhythm and notice how comfortable it is. Allow yourself to enjoy full inhalations of breath and feel your heart reaching upwards to the Angels as you do.

4. Call upon Archangel Gabriel, the Angel of Empowerment, to be with you and know that your call to her is responded to immediately. Archangel Gabriel is with you now.

5. Imagine Gabriel is surrounding you with her loving, golden and white aura and radiating empowering truth. Notice how the energy around you feels so uplifted and optimistic now.

6. Imagine Archangel Gabriel placing her hand over your heart and feel the appreciation of

your heart as it responds to Gabriel's energy. Feel your heart, your place of Love, remembering the Love that you have for yourself.

7. Focus on an area of your life in which you would like to be empowered, more honest and truthful.

8. Imagine Archangel Gabriel's hand draw any difficult feelings away from you and replacing those feelings with honesty, integrity and empowerment. Notice your heart becoming lighter.

9. Focus on the area of your life in which you would like to be more honest and truthful and see if filled with Gabriel's golden light of empowerment.

10. Thank Archangel Gabriel for helping you to accept the empowerment of honesty into your life.

An Angelic Card Exercise for You to Enjoy

Take a moment to read about Oracle Card Reading on page 7 before you begin.

As you have seen in Chapter 4, Archangel Gabriel encourages you to nourish your soul by allowing yourself to take time away from all of the rush and pressure and problems you feel part of, and take a walk by yourself, find a place to be still and quiet. Listen to your needs. Honor and value yourself first, then give to your family all of the true Love you experience from yourself. Enjoy your friends from a place of equality and honesty.

Take your Oracle Cards in your hands and fill them with Love and all that Love means to you. Allow your cards to become warmed by your hands. Gently shuffle your cards and take your time and enjoy your connection with them. Anticipate clarity and Love from your cards; expect them to help you and they will.

When you are ready, ask the Archangel Gabriel:

'Archangel Gabriel, please provide me with your loving guidance'

Now choose a card for each of the questions below.

Note down the cards as you choose them and what you feel that they are conveying to you.

1. What is it that Archangel Gabriel would like to communicate to me today?

2. How can I begin to truthfully listen to my own needs?

3. How can I more easily *identify* my own needs?

4. How can I *release* any limitations to having my needs met?

And when you have finished, thank Archangel Gabriel for her help by simply saying 'Thank you'.

Archangel Gabriel

My Thoughts, Feelings and Requests

This is the very special place for you to record your thoughts and feelings. Use this very special place to ask the Angels to help you with anything which you become aware of or would like to ask for, as you move through the chapters of this book.

Chapter Five

Archangel Raphael

Chapter Five

Archangel Raphael

By the end of this chapter you will:

- ❤ Have called Archangel Raphael to be with you with an Angelic Invocation

- ❤ Understand how Archangel Raphael can help you to improve your life

- ❤ Have received Archangel Raphael's help to make more healthful choices in your life

- ❤ Have received Archangel Raphael's further guidance and advice with Oracle Cards

Archangel Raphael Invocation

Take a moment to read about invocations on page 5 before you begin.

It's time to connect with the Angelic Realm now and to call Archangel Raphael to be with you. So, close your eyes and give yourself permission for this experience.

Now, take some relaxing breaths and gently focus your intention and full expectation upon connecting with Archangel Raphael.

It is your intention and expectation to connect with the Archangel of Healing which will allow your channel of Angelic communication to become open.

And now ask Archangel Raphael to be with you.

Archangel Raphael is with you right now.

Open your heart to his safe, secure and loving aura.

Feel with all of your senses and see in your mind's eye, the crystal clear, emerald green aura of Archangel Raphael.

Ask him to surround you with his limitlessly healing energy and ask him to direct it to your emotions, your body and your soul.

Ask Raphael to help you to experience his healing through your whole life by helping you to make healthy and positive choices in all areas of your life.

Now spend some time, becoming more familiar with Raphael's energy.

Ask Archangel Raphael to help you to recognise his energy every time he is near you.

Ask that Raphael stay with you throughout this chapter. And so it is.

Well Done! You have now begun a wonderful relationship with Archangel Raphael, the Healing Angel, a bond that will remain with you throughout the whole of your life. Raphael will come to you every time you call him, instantly and without fail - and remember, just because your awareness of him may still be subtle, it does not mean that his presence is any less true.

How Will You Experience Archangel Raphael's Presence?

You might see Archangel Raphael's emerald green light, feel his deeply healing energy around you, hear Raphael's words of loving wellbeing and healthful support or just know that Raphael is with you because of the deep sense of wellbeing he brings to you. Honour and value your communication channel with him and know that it is perfect for you.

How Can Archangel Raphael Help Me?

Archangel Raphael is the Healing Archangel who embodies and radiates the energy of healing and wellbeing. His crystal clear emerald green aura radiates a powerful healing light to all those who call upon him.

Self Forgiveness and Compassion

Archangel Raphael will help us to enjoy the health and wellbeing we access when we learn how to forgive. To forgive is to be *free*. It is to release any energy, thoughts, feelings or memories which weigh you down. It is to release anger, a sense of injustice or the feeling that you are a perpetual victim. To forgive is to take responsibility for your own feelings, and realize that you and no one else decide how you feel.

Forgiveness is a process, and there are times in your life when you will be ready to let go of how you feel and there will be times when you are not. For those times when you are ready, your need to be right or superior or justified dissolves, letting Love and compassion take their place. You'll then be able to see the price you have been paying for carrying around reminders of how bad something was, or how bad you were made to feel.

Raphael has often explained to me that forgiveness is nothing to do with how justified you are to feel as you do. It has nothing to do with how many people agree that something was wrong, or who can add to your negative strength of feeling, by pointing out the unfairness of it. Instead, it has everything to do with the realisation that it is Love you wish to feel and experience in your life, and that you are the gatekeeper to this Love.

To forgive does not mean that you weren't hurt or that it didn't happen or that it didn't matter. It doesn't mean that you were right and they were wrong. What it does mean is that Love is more important to you than anything else. When you allow yourself the gift of forgiveness, by forgiving others and forgiving yourself, you are allowing your wounds to heal and allowing wellbeing to reach you as never before. Forgiveness is good for your health!

Helping Those Who Heal Others

Archangel Raphael will work with you if you wish to become a channel for his healing power. He will help you to heal yourself and others so that everyone can experience wellbeing in their lives. He will help you to find your own unique and personal way of working energetically with others, and supporting your healing path.

Sending Wellbeing

Archangel Raphael explains that when you want to help another by sending them healing, you send them the quality you wish them to receive. Don't send them worry or concern, or think about their pain or diagnosis. Instead send them wellbeing and health, strength and, vitality, comfort and Love.

Take a moment: *Ask Raphael to surround your loved one with the energy and qualities which you feel will help them the most at this time. Know that it is done instantly and constantly. At times of need, you can also ask Archangel Raphael to stay with your loved one and be with them at all times.*

Visualising Wellbeing

Raphael asks that when you think of another in any situation, focus on a vision of their wellbeing. It is easy to talk about other people's problems, and try to solve their problems for them by discussing their difficulties, but your efforts to help, will, quite inadvertently, add focus and energy to their difficulties. Archangel Raphael tells us that when we want to heal another it is important to think of the quality or the resolution you wish the recipient to experience. If a loved one is sick, think of them as vital and well, if they have problems with their life, think of them as having the courage and strength to solve them. It is this approach which will bring real benefit to your loved one and to you too.

Healing for Past Lives

Archangel Raphael can help heal the wounds of past life experiences. Throughout history, light workers have experienced unspeakable harm for their beliefs and gifts, and the resulting fear and pain can follow us through many incarnations. It is very often the case that if you are drawn to working with the light in this life, you had the same desire to do so in previous incarnations, and probably at a time when your gift was not understood. Archangel Raphael will help heal these wounds and release you from the fear that is carried within them.

Healing Relationships

Archangel Raphael can be called upon to bring healing to difficult or challenging relationships, and to provide balance and harmony to all those concerned. He will help you open your heart so you can experience true happiness and contentment. He will help you to offer the Love from your heart that will allow you to receive the Love from your life.

Chapter 5 – Visualisation

Archangel Raphael

Realignment with Complete Wellbeing

The purpose of this visualisation is to allow every part of you to be touched by the powerful healing energy of Archangel Raphael. Through Raphael you will experience physical and emotional wellbeing and the limitless supply of Universal balance, internal harmony and vibrant good health which is your birthright.

1. Sit quietly with your eyes closed and relax your body. Place your hands gently in your lap with your palms facing upwards. Imagine your whole body relaxing and becoming physically comfortable.

2. Give this Angelic experience to yourself as vital nourishment. Award yourself this nourishing act of improvement which will allow you to enjoy wellbeing in all areas of your life.

3. Become aware of your breath and allow your focus to gently come to rest with your own rhythm and notice how comfortable it is. Allow yourself to enjoy full inhalations of breath and feel your heart reaching upwards to the Angels as you do.

4. Call upon Archangel Raphael, the Angel of Healing and Wellbeing, to be with you and know that your call to him is responded to immediately. Archangel Raphael is with you now.

5. Imagine Raphael is surrounding you with his emerald green healing light. Notice how the energy around you feels so vibrant and charged with life.

6. Imagine Archangel Raphael's emerald green healing light reaching your body. Feel how gratefully your body receives Archangel Raphael's healing energy. Feel how thirsty your body has been for Archangel Raphael's health giving energy and light. Feel how deeply your body is absorbing Archangel Raphael's healing energy.

7. Imagine that Archangel Raphael is filling your whole physical body from the tips of your toes to the top of your head, from the deepest part of you, to the surface of your skin, and from every atom of your being, to the organs which rely upon their existence, with beautiful, healing, energizing and health giving emerald green light.

8. Imagine Archangel Raphael's emerald green healing light reaching your emotions. Feel the appreciation of your emotions. Feel how thirsty your emotions have been to experience the peace and harmony of Archangel Raphael's healing light.

9. Archangel Raphael now fills all of your emotions from your past to your present and into your bright new future with his balancing, harmonious, peaceful and health giving emerald green light. Allow yourself to receive this healing light as never before and accept emotional wellbeing.

10. Return to the room glowing, feeling recharged, vital and alive with Archangel Raphael's healing energy.

11. Thank Archangel Raphael for helping you to experience physical and emotional wellbeing and healing.

An Angelic Card Exercise for You to Enjoy

Take a moment to read about Oracle Card Reading on page 7 before you begin.

As you have seen in Chapter 5, working with Archangel Raphael will help you to experience increased well being in all areas of your life. The Angels will help you in many ways by empowering you to take positive action and Archangel Raphael will help you make healthful choices in your life which will help you to heal. It is now time to ask Archangel Raphael to provide you with his guidance and further insight through Oracle Cards.

Take your Oracle Cards in your hands and fill them with Love and all that Love means to you. Allow your cards to become warmed by your hands. Gently shuffle your cards and take your time and enjoy your connection with them. Anticipate clarity and Love from your cards; expect them to help you and they will.

When you are ready, ask the Archangel Raphael:

'Archangel Raphael, please provide me with your loving guidance'

Now choose a card for each of the questions below.

Note down the cards as you choose them and what you feel that they are conveying to you.

1. What is it that Archangel Raphael would like to communicate to me today?

2. How can I experience more health in my life?

3. How can I *identify* the parts of me which are ready to be healed?

4. How can I *release* any issues or energy which restrict my flow of wellbeing?

And when you have finished, thank Archangel Raphael for his help by simply saying 'Thank you'.

Archangel Raphael

My Thoughts, Feelings and Requests

This is the very special place for you to record your thoughts and feelings. Use this very special place to ask the Angels to help you with anything which you become aware of or would like to ask for, as you move through the chapters of this book.

Chapter Six

Archangel Chamuel

Chapter Six

Archangel Chamuel

By the end of this chapter you will:

- ❤ Have called Archangel Chamuel to be with you with an Angelic Invocation

- ❤ Understand how Archangel Chamuel can help you to improve your life

- ❤ Have received Archangel Chamuel's help to love and appreciate yourself more

- ❤ Have received Archangel Chamuel's further guidance and advice with Oracle Cards

Archangel Chamuel Invocation

Take a moment to read about invocations on page 5 before you begin.

It's time to connect with the Angelic Realm now and to call Archangel Chamuel to be with you. So, close your eyes and give yourself permission for this experience.

Now, take some relaxing breaths and gently focus your intention and full expectation upon connecting with Archangel Chamuel.

It is your intention and expectation to connect with the Archangel of Love which will allow your channel of Angelic communication to become open.

And now ask Archangel Chamuel to be with you.

Archangel Chamuel is with you right now.

Open your heart to his safe, secure and loving aura.

Feel with all of your senses and see in your mind's eye, the beautiful, tender pink aura of Archangel Chamuel.

Ask him to surround you with his limitless and unconditional Love. Ask him to direct his Love to your emotions, your body and your soul. Ask Chamuel to help you to experience his Love throughout your whole life. Ask him to help you to open your heart is unconditional and accepting Love.

Now spend some time, becoming more familiar with Chamuel's energy.

Ask Archangel Chamuel to help you to recognise his energy every time he is near you.

Ask that Chamuel stay with you throughout this chapter.

And so it is.

Well Done! You have now begun a wonderful relationship with Archangel Chamuel the Archangel of Love and established a bond which will help you in more and more ways as each day passes. Each time you call, Archangel Chamuel will come to your side instantly, with his eternal Love and never ending compassion.

How Will You Experience Archangel Chamuel's Presence?

To reveal his presence in your life, Archangel Chamuel may allow you to experience more Love in your life by opening your ears to hear kind and loving words. He may direct your attention to songs on the radio which speak to your heart, or use everyday events to show you that he is there. He may help you notice the soft, pink scarf of a friend, the generosity of heart and spirit in others, or kind offers of help. He may help you take advantage of opportunities to demonstrate your unconditional Love and acceptance of others. Remember, you will always find evidence of the Angels in your life if you are looking for it.

Take a moment: *Feel how Archangel Chamuel is communicating with you today. Do you feel him with you now? Because he is. Do you see his tender pink, soothing aura? Do you feel his loving and accepting energy around you? Do you know that Chamuel is with you because of the way your heart feels? Embrace and bathe in whichever way you notice Chamuel's presence in your life, no matter how subtle.*

How Can Archangel Chamuel Help You?

Archangel Chamuel is the Angel of Love and he encourages us to Love and appreciate ourselves more. He helps us to experience more Love in our lives in all its forms. He has told me on many occasions that Love is the only thing that is real –

that everything else is interpretation or perception or opinion. Everything.

Love is the most powerful energy in the whole Universe. Surely that is worth having more of in our lives?

You Are So Easy to Love

It was Archangel Chamuel who explained to me that the Angels see us as pure Love and beauty, as a beautiful shining light which encapsulates the Love energy of everyone we've ever loved, and everyone who has ever loved us. The light shines brightly with the energy that's generated from every time we've ever smiled or laughed, and every drop of happiness and positivity that we have experienced in our lives. Archangel Chamuel encourages you to see yourself though the eyes of the Angels, so that you can understand how easy you are to Love.

Love Begins with You

Loving yourself is one of the most important life lessons that you are here to learn. Loving yourself is where your happiness begins and ends. Once you have learnt how to Love yourself, you will find that positive and enriching experiences can reach you in ways you could never have imagined.

Archangel Chamuel will help you to love yourself more by opening your eyes to your true beauty and by helping you to accept your true value. You are so loved by all the Angels, so treasured and cherished. Chamuel will help you to be kinder to yourself and to treat yourself with great tenderness and compassion. He will help you to understand yourself and learn how to show yourself that you care.

He will also help you to see your gifts, and to accept what makes you special. He will transform your limiting view of yourself by providing you with opportunities to see the Love and positivity that is always present in your life. Here, Archangel Chamuel works closely with Archangel Jophiel to help you see the beauty of your world and every-one and everything in it. Tenderness, kindness, compassion, appreciation, laughter, joy will all be shown to you if you allow yourself to see them.

Chamuel tells us that we will always find what we are looking for in our lives. If we are always looking for Love, imagine how much we will find.

Healing Relationships with Love

Archangel Chamuel will work powerfully to heal relationships which have been damaged in the past and also, to enhance current relationships. He will help you to welcome into your life the positive changes and improvements which always accompany Love.

Love in All Its Forms

Love has many different forms and expresses itself in thousands of ways. Love can enhance all areas of your life if it is only allowed in. Be clear about the kind of Love you would like to experience. Feel it, ask Archangel Chamuel to bring it to you, then give yourself permission to receive it.

Chamuel can increase the flow of Love in your life in many ways and many forms. He can help you to find new and positive people to enrich your experiences; meet new friends, create more meaningful relationships and discover your soul mate - Chamuel encourages you not to wait! *Feel* Love now, *see* Love now, *welcome* Love now and expect to find it. Don't wait for someone to come into your life to show you what Love is, because nobody knows better than you do what Love means to you.

You'll Always Find What You're Looking For

Archangel Chamuel's message is that you will always find what we are looking for in your life. Pay attention to what you are asking for with your feelings. Are you asking for more Love, or are you actually feeling the fear of rejection? Are you asking for more Love, or are you actually feeling that you will always be alone? Are you asking for more Love, or are you feeling closed and negative? *Feel* the Love in your life that you would like to discover and you will be brought it in many thousands of ways.

Opening Your Heart Centre

Archangel Chamuel will help you to blossom, unfurl and bathe in the Love that exists in the very air that you breathe, in a way which feels perfect to you. He will help you to open your heart - an entirely positive experience that will enable you to become a magnet to Love in many wonderful ways. Opening your heart means allowing yourself to feel warmth and softness, and to lay down your defences. It's a strong and empowered path full of happiness which allows you to see the illusions that egos and personalities create. Living your life with an open heart allows you to know that all is well, that you are part of a benevolent Universe that is working *with* you and always has been.

Ask Archangel Chamuel to help you to choose a path of openness and Love and he will help you find your way to your very own paradise.

Chapter 6 – Visualisation

Archangel Chamuel

Enhancing My Relationships with Love

The purpose of this visualisation is to help you to experience more Love in your relationships.

Before you begin, think of a loved one you would like to love more; a loved one that you would like to be closer to. Think of a loved one that you would like to have a more understanding, feeling, sensitive and compassionate relationship with.

You may choose to work with a partner, a husband or wife, a child, a sibling, a parent, a close friend or anyone you would like to love more.

Write their name here:

_____

1. Sit quietly with your eyes closed and relax your body. Place your hands gently in your lap with your palms facing upwards. Imagine your whole body relaxing and becoming physically comfortable.

2. Give this Angelic experience to yourself as a beautiful step towards positive change. Allow yourself the improvement which this experience will bring to you, and to your relationships.

3. Become aware of your breath and allow your focus to gently come to rest with your own rhythm and notice how comfortable it is. Allow yourself to enjoy full inhalations of breath and feel your heart reaching upwards to the Angels as you do.

4. Call upon Archangel Chamuel, the Angel of Love, to be with you and know that your call to him is responded to immediately. Archangel Chamuel is with you now.

5. Imagine Chamuel is surrounding you with his tender, loving soft pink aura and filling you with Love and compassion.

6. Bring into your mind now the loved one you would like to love more and greet them warmly.

7. Think of the qualities of Love you would like to experience in your relationship. Think of affection, tenderness, understanding, warmth, intimacy or any other quality of Love you would like to bring into your relationship.

8. Imagine Archangel Chamuel sending to you a deep sense of that loving quality you have chosen. He will help you to feel the feelings you want to experience in your relationship and identify those loving feelings within yourself.

9. Imagine facing your loved one now and allow all of the positive feelings and qualities of Love that you are experiencing, to flow to them. Feel your heart softening and becoming warm and loving as you radiate to your loved one the beautiful essence of all the feelings which you wish to experience in your relationship.

10. Thank Archangel Chamuel for helping you to experience more Love in your relationship.

An Angelic Card Exercise for You to Enjoy

Take a moment to read about Oracle Card Reading on page 7 before you begin.

As you have seen in Chapter 6, Archangel Chamuel will help you to attract more Love into your life in all its forms. He will help you to become more open and loving and to he will teach you how to feel the Love you are asking for. It is now time to ask Archangel Chamuel to provide you with his guidance and further insight through Oracle Cards.

Take your Oracle Cards in your hands and fill them with Love and all that Love means to you. Allow your cards to become warmed by your hands. Gently shuffle your cards and take your time and enjoy your connection with them. Anticipate clarity and Love from your cards; expect them to help you and they will.

When you are ready, ask the Archangel Chamuel:

'Archangel Chamuel, please provide me with your loving guidance'

Now choose a card for each of the questions below.

Note down the cards as you choose them and what you feel that they are conveying to you.

1. What is it that Archangel Chamuel would like to communicate to me today?

2. How can I open my heart to more Love?

3. How can I *identify* more reasons to love and appreciate myself?

4. How can I *release* any thoughts or beliefs about myself which restrict my ability to love and appreciate myself more?

And when you have finished, thank Archangel Chamuel for his help by simply saying 'Thank you'.

Archangel Chamuel

My Thoughts, Feelings and Requests

This is the very special place for you to record your thoughts and feelings. Use this very special place to ask the Angels to help you with anything which you become aware of or would like to ask for, as you move through the chapters of this book.

Chapter Seven

Archangel Zadkiel

Chapter Seven

Archangel Zadkiel

By the end of this chapter you will:

- ❤ Have called Archangel Zadkiel to be with you with an Angelic Invocation

- ❤ Understand how Archangel Zadkiel can help you to improve your life

- ❤ Have received Archangel Zadkiel's help to forgive yourself

- ❤ Have received Archangel Zadkiel's further guidance and advice with Oracle Cards

Archangel Zadkiel Invocation

Take a moment to read about invocations on page 5 before you begin.

It's time to connect with the Angelic Realm now and to call Archangel Zadkiel to be with you. So, close your eyes and give yourself permission for this experience.

Now, take some relaxing breaths and gently focus your intention and full expectation upon connecting with Archangel Zadkiel.

It is your intention and expectation to connect with Archangel Zadkiel, the Angel of the Violet Flame, which will allow your channel of Angelic communication to become open.

And now ask Archangel Zadkiel to be with you.

Archangel Zadkiel is with you right now.

Open your heart to his safe, secure and loving aura.

Feel with all of your senses and see in your mind's eye, the deep purple with golden flecks of light that is the Archangel Zadkiel.

Ask him to surround you with his rich and abundant energy. Ask Archangel Zadkiel to help you to make more space in your life for all the gifts of the Universe. Do that now.

Now spend some time, becoming more familiar with Zadkiel's energy.

Ask Zadkiel to help you to recognise his energy every time he is near you.

Ask that Archangel Zadkiel stay with you throughout this chapter.

And so it is.

Well done! You are on a wonderful Angelic journey - allow yourself to enjoy every step of the way. Remember that your very own way of communicating with the Archangels is being developed now. Every time you ask an Archangel to be with you, they will come and every time this happens your awareness of their energy will become a little stronger. Your intention and continued expectation of feeling the Archangels will see it become a natural part of your life.

How Will You Experience Archangel Zadkiel's Presence?

Archangel Zadkiel is the Archangel of Transformation, and works powerfully with the Violet Flame of Transmutation. He is also known as the Bringer of Joy, and helps us to understand how to attract more of the things which give us pleasure. Zadkiel radiates a powerful, deep purple aura, flecked with golden sparkles of positivity, and you may see these colours as a way of knowing that Zadkiel is with you. It may be that Zadkiel's light and colours will appear in your life through a rich purple scarf or even jewellery worn by you or others. Zadkiel may help you to feel that he is with you, by making you aware of your readiness to let go of past arguments and misunderstandings. Be open to the many hundreds of ways that Archangel Zadkiel will enter your life - and appreciate them all for the positivity they bring.

How Can Archangel Zadkiel Help Me?

Archangel Zadkiel helps us to exchange any limitations we have imposed on ourselves for abundance and all the gifts of the Universe. His aura contains an energy of enormous positivity, and he brings great joy and upliftment whenever he is present. Zadkiel constantly reminds us of the enormous benefit of feeling joy in our life *as it is.* By allowing ourselves to see and feel the wonder contained in our lives already, we give our permission for the Angels to bring us more things we love and enjoy.

The Angel of the Violet Flame

Archangel Zadkiel works with the Violet Flame of Transmutation, an unimaginable energetic force able to dissolve all negativity. Zadkiel offers to take all of the negativity in your life however it manifests itself – be it, anger, frustration, resentment or fear. He will help you manifest positivity in your life in thousands of ways, through Love. He will help you to manifest positivity through abundance, pleasure and enjoyment, through health, laughter and smiles.

To the Angels, positivity simply means all the good things in life, all the things that make us feel blessed and smiled upon.

When you feel positively from inside of yourself and have positive expectations about your life, and know that the Angels and the Universe are working *with* you, you are allowing the flow of all good things to reach you. You will find that suddenly you have access to the incredible flow of Universal Abundance - a limitless, benevolent stream of energy which offers you everything you want and need, to flourish and grow.

When this happens, you will have stepped out of your *own way* and let go of all of the negativity and fear. You will have realised the value of perceiving your life in a way that *benefits* you. And *that* is how you begin to ask the Angels to bring you what you *really* want.

Negativity Repels Abundance

Negativity constricts the flow of Universal abundance to you; no matter how subtle you consider it to be or how deep you have buried it inside yourself. Negativity has nothing to do with how justified you are to feel the way you do, how wrong the other person was or how unfair or challenging your situation is. Negativity is a detrimental energy which prevents you from accessing the limitless supply of abundance which the Universe has to offer you.

Negativity pretends to be our friend; it agrees with all our problems and tells us how right we are to feel the unhelpful emotions we do. It justifies our reasons to blame other people, our bad luck, our misfortune, and it tells us to expect the worst. Negativity provides us with the proof we need to stay closed and fearful, and it hangs on until the bitter end to prove how right it was. Some friend!

Your negativity may come in the form of anger, resentment, needing to be right, shame, judging others, feeling sorry for yourself, hating the situation you find yourself in, blaming everything and everyone else for your problems and hundreds more self-sabotaging feelings and emotions. Remember, y*ou* prevent Universal Abundance from reaching you, and you control the flow. Universal Abundance has never decided *not* to come and be with you, and it's always waiting to join you.

You Control the Flow

Preventing Universal Abundance from reaching you is like having your foot placed firmly over a hose pipe with the tap full on at the wall. You're staring into the end of the hose, wondering where all your water is.

All you need to do is take your foot off the hose pipe and you will have water again. Just because you can't see any water, it doesn't mean it's not there. You know it's there. You know the tap is on.

The Angels and the Universe are *always* working with you to bring you what you are asking for from life but *what* is it you are asking for? Do you know? Can you feel the *positivity* of all of the wonderful things that you would like to fill your life with? Or can you feel the *negativity* of the problems or the lack of things you want? And which do you feel most strongly? This is how much of your flow are you restricting. Just take your foot off.

Your Desires Require No Justification

There is a belief here on earth that some desires are more 'worthy' than others. There is belief that to desire money or possessions or wealth is somehow less spiritual. This is not the Angels' perception; they do not judge your desires or question your requests.

Archangel Zadkiel asks you to consider what it is about possessions that you really want as this is how you will manifest. Wanting money, for example, may mean you want to feel more independent, secure, self-sufficient and independent, or you may want lots of money to provide you with the sense of success that you feel you are lacking. Become aware of the energy and qualities which your material desires contain and you will manifest accurately.

Archangel Zadkiel has explained to me that it is necessary for you to work out what it is that a new home, new car, more money or a fantastic new wardrobe of clothes actually *means* to you. What are the feelings which you associate or connect with the objects of your desire?

In order for you to experience the things you want in your life, you don't need to demonstrate to the Angels how much you deserve them, you just need identify and connect with the feeling you think you will have when these desires are fulfilled. You need to feel the way you will feel when you have them. Imagine they have already arrived and feel as you would having them, before they appear.

Archangel Zadkiel explains that by approaching your life in this way, you will transform your present and be able to manifest your future easily and enjoyably.

Releasing from Your Heart without Fear

Archangel Zadkiel will help you to release any heaviness and negative energy which you hold within your heart, and he will help you to stop punishing yourself. Zadkiel lovingly tells you that you have *outgrown* negative ways of reacting to the world, and that it is time for you to do things differently. Be the change you want to see.

By releasing the negative thoughts and distractions which prevent you from accessing the flow of Universal Abundance which you are always connected to, you will attract the abundant, joyful, happy, satisfying and fulfilling life that you are waiting for.

Take a moment: *Begin to do things differently and attract positive change by saying:*

'Archangel Zadkiel, Angel of Transformation and the Violet Flame, I now offer you all of the negativity that I have held onto in my life, in all its forms. I release to you any negativity in whatever form it is manifest, be it unforgiveness, anger, resentment or fear, as I understand it constricts the flow of Universal abundance to me. I ask that you take all negative energy from me and replace it with positivity and Love.' And so it is.

Chapter 7 – Visualisation

Archangel Zadkiel

Allowing the Flow of Universal Abundance

The purpose of this visualisation is to release any negative thoughts and memories, behaviours or emotions as well as any unforgiveness that you hold in your heart towards yourself or any other person.

Archangel Zadkiel will help you to allow Universal Abundance into your life. Allowing Universal Abundance to reach you is the same as allowing yourself to receive; it's the same as allowing yourself to accept it, allowing yourself to notice it, allowing yourself to identify it, allowing yourself to embrace it and allowing yourself to become friends with abundance again. The Universe has always been your friend and always will be.

1. Sit quietly with your eyes closed and relax your body. Place your hands gently in your lap with your palms facing upwards. Imagine your whole body relaxing and becoming physically comfortable.

2. Give this Angelic experience to yourself as a gift. Allow yourself the abundance of all good things which this experience will bring to you, and to your whole life

3. Become aware of your breath and allow your focus to gently come to rest with your own rhythm and notice how comfortable it is. Allow yourself to enjoy full inhalations of breath and feel your heart reaching upwards to the Angels as you do.

4. Call upon Archangel Zadkiel, the Angel of Transformation, to be with you and know that your call to him is responded to immediately. Archangel Zadkiel is with you now.

5. Imagine Zadkiel is surrounding you with his loving and transformational violet aura now and filling you with positivity and Love.

6. Imagine Archangel Zadkiel standing directly in front of you holding his cupped hands out towards you. Archangel Zadkiel asks you to allow yourself this opportunity to release any negativity or unforgiveness that you are holding onto.

7. Archangel Zadkiel asks you to begin by forgiving *yourself.* Forgive yourself for any and all negative things you may have said, ways you may have acted and all of the critical thoughts that you have about yourself. Forgive yourself for your self-doubt, forgive yourself for your fear, and forgive yourself for your intolerances and your judgments.

8. Release all of the negative feelings as they come to you, and place them in Archangel Zadkiel's cupped hands.

9. Imagine that every part of you is releasing now, and that Love and abundance are taking the place of negativity and unforgiveness. Feel how brightly you are shining. Feel how much clearer and lighter you are. Feel your connection to Love and abundance of all good things now.

10. Thank Archangel Zadkiel for helping you to release negativity and for filling that space with positivity and abundance.

An Angelic Card Exercise for You to Enjoy

Take a moment to read about Oracle Card Reading on page 7 before you begin.

As you have seen in Chapter 7, Archangel Zadkiel will exchange any negativity in your life, for positivity and abundance. It is now time to ask Archangel Zadkiel to provide you with his guidance and further insight through Oracle Cards.

Take your Oracle Cards in your hands and fill them with Love and all that Love means to you. Allow your cards to become warmed by your hands. Gently shuffle your cards and take your time and enjoy your connection with them. Anticipate clarity and Love from your cards; expect them to help you and they will.

When you are ready, ask the Archangel Zadkiel:

'Archangel Zadkiel, please provide me with your loving guidance'

Now choose a card for each of the questions below.

Note down the cards as you choose them and what you feel that they are conveying to you.

1. What is it that Archangel Zadkiel would like to communicate to me today?

2. What is the most positive step that I can take today to attract more positivity into my life?

3. How can I *identify* the forms of negativity I have in my life?

4. How can I *release* the forms of negativity I have in my life?

And when you have finished, thank Archangel Zadkiel for his help by simply saying 'Thank you'.

Archangel Zadkiel

My Thoughts, Feelings and Requests

This is the very special place for you to record your thoughts and feelings. Use this very special place to ask the Angels to help you with anything which you become aware of or would like to ask for, as you move through the chapters of this book.

Chapter Eight

Archangel Metatron

Chapter Eight

Archangel Metatron

By the end of this chapter you will:

- ♥ Have called Archangel Metatron to be with you with an Angelic Invocation

- ♥ Understand how Archangel Metatron can help you to improve your life

- ♥ Have received Archangel Metatron's help to take inspired action in your life

- ♥ Have received Archangel Metatron's further guidance and advice with Oracle Cards

Archangel Metatron Invocation

Take a moment to read about invocations on page 5 before you begin.

It's time to connect with the Angelic Realm now and to call Archangel Metatron to be with you. So, close your eyes and give yourself permission for this experience.

Now, take some relaxing breaths and gently focus your intention and full expectation upon connecting with Archangel Metatron, the Angel of Inspiration and Motivation.

It is your intention and expectation to connect with Metatron, which will allow your channel of Angelic communication to become open. Do that now.

And now ask Archangel Metatron to be with you.

Archangel Metatron is with you right now.

Open your heart to his safe, secure and loving aura.

Feel with all of your senses and see in your mind's eye, the powerful silver, golden and violet aura of Archangel Metatron.

Ask him to surround you with his energy of inspiration and motivation. Ask him to help you to take the action needed in your life to bring you positive outcomes in all areas.

Ask him to bring an energy of positive movement into your body, your mind and into every part of your life.

Now spend some time, becoming more familiar with Metatron's energy.

Ask Archangel Metatron to help you to recognise his energy every time he is near you.

Ask that Archangel Metatron stay with you throughout this chapter. And so it is.

Well Done! You have now begun a wonderful relationship with Archangel Metatron, the Archangel of Inspiration.

As you have learnt now, the Archangels will show you that they are there if you look for them. You may feel, see, sense or just know that Archangel Metatron has entered your life and believe me, your life will never be the same again.

How Will You Experience Archangel Metatron's Presence?

Ask Archangel Metatron to show you his presence in your life, and look for his motivational energy and inspiring influence. He has an incredible aura of silver gold and violet, and he radiates the energy to create Miracles. Metatron will offer you the words of much needed inspiration in your ear, his voice will remind you that you can do it, and his energy will motivate you to meet your toughest challenges and to be in awe of your personal victories.

Metatron may help you to know that he is with you, by directing you to inspiring books or bringing people into your life who motivate you with their words and actions. Metatron may show you that he is with you, by giving you the willpower you need to achieve a goal or complete a task. He may drop exciting ideas into your mind and help you to take positive steps towards making your ideas reality.

Archangel Metatron may wake you up in the morning with an excited feeling about something good you know is coming or he may help you to take just one step at a time toward positive change.

How Can Archangel Metatron Help Me?

Archangel Metatron is known as the Archangel of Inspiration and Motivation, and also as the Leader of Children. Together with his spiritual brother, Archangel Sandalphon, he's the only Archangel ever to have lived a mortal life. Metatron is so aware of our human challenges here on earth – he is so in touch with what it is to be human but from a completely Angelic perspective. He seems to have retained the earthly knowledge he gained through his experiences here, and his memories allow him a great understanding and empathy. He sees the world from the perspective of the Archangels, but also has an appreciation of what it is like to be human.

Because of this Metatron is brilliant at helping us with some of our fundamental human faults. He can help you conquer procrastination, to see that in life there really is no right or wrong, and to learn how become responsible and proactive.

Archangel Metatron and Children

Archangel Metatron is often referred to as the Leader of Children, and he helps every child and young person on Earth and in Heaven achieve person greatness. To adults, children often appear to exist in another world. Children play, think, experiment and interact with their environment in a way which is open and free, learning and developing as they do. Every day is exciting, fresh and new to them, and they are full of the joy of life. Archangel Metatron reminds us to be inspired by our children, or 'young lightworkers' as he calls them.

A child's memory of where they came from before they were born is often still very strong. They will often remember past lives or who they were 'before', and will also know the Source energy they came from. Children will sometimes talk about the 'choice' they made to come to the physical family they are now part of, and can stare into the space around a person to see their aura and energy field. They laugh and chatter to unseen guides and loving energies, and continue their 'studies' as they sleep, when they are taught and told wonderful Universal secrets by the Angels and their guides.

Archangel Metatron will support the relationship between children and adults, and help them understand each other. Children have so much to offer to adults.

Archangel Metatron has explained to me that children will look for the Love of Source from their parents, their wider family, their friends, their siblings and from all of their experiences. They still remember the Love of Source and search for it. Children need to know that they are loved – however they behave. To withdraw Love is to withdraw their Source energy and their reference to where they came from. They will be lost without Love, and will not know where or who they are. Metatron reminds us that we have all been children at some time in our lives, and that we are always children in our hearts.

Releasing the Need to Judge

Archangel Metatron reminds us that judging others and ourselves is futile. He reminds us that there is no right and wrong in life, and that each of us approaches life from different experiences and perspectives.

It isn't often possible to understand why others act as they do, why they make choices we don't agree with and why they can't see the world in the same way that we do. But Archangel Metatron will help you understand that it isn't necessary to make sense of another person's life, and that when you release your judgments, you will free yourself from the fear that you are judged by others. Releasing the need to judge allows you to focus on your own life.

Conquering Overwhelming Tasks and Emotions

Archangel Metatron can be called upon at any time you feel overwhelmed. When a task seems impossible he will provide whatever quality or energy you need to complete it. Archangel Metatron will direct motivation, inspiration, productivity, application, perseverance, focus, action and very often miracles into the area of your life which needs his energy.

Metatron will also help you find balance and evenness in your emotions. When strong and overwhelming emotions well up inside of us, threatening to blind and paralyse us, Archangel Metatron can be called upon to help us find our centre of gravity again and approach our life in a more comfortable and enjoyable way.

If ever you feel overwhelmed by anything in your life, call upon Archangel Metatron and say,

'Archangel Metatron, please bring balance into my life and provide me with the sense of self that I need in order to find my centre of peace.'

Action and Pro-Activity

Archangel Metatron is the Angel to call upon if you tend to procrastinate or delay taking action. He will help you make decisions, and follow a course of action through to its satisfying completion. Archangel Metatron will help you to act positively and effectively, so you can experience the feelings of significance and sense of contribution which you will gain so much from in life.

Chapter 8 – Visualisation

Archangel Metatron

Feeling Motivation and Inspiration

The purpose of this visualisation is to help you to remember how it feels to be inspired and excited by your life. Archangel Metatron will help you to approach your whole life from a new and fresh perspective and be inspired into action again.

If you are ready to be motivated, inspired and excited about your life again, Archangel Metatron will help you.

1. Sit quietly with your eyes closed and relax your body. Place your hands gently in your lap with your palms facing upwards. Imagine your whole body relaxing and becoming physically comfortable.

2. Give this Angelic experience to yourself as a gift. Allow yourself to benefit from the motivational and inspirational energy of Archangel Metatron and commit to your own success.

3. Become aware of your breath and allow your focus to gently come to rest with your own rhythm and notice how comfortable it is. Allow yourself to enjoy full inhalations of breath and feel your heart reaching upwards to the Angels as you do.

4. Call upon Archangel Metatron, the Angel of Motivation and Inspiration, to be with you and know that your call to him is responded to immediately. Archangel Metatron is with you now.

5. Imagine Metatron is surrounding you with his incredible golden, silver and violet aura and filling you with a deep sense of what you know you can achieve in your life.

6. Think of a colour which represents inspiration to you. A colour which represents excitement and enthusiasm to you. A colour which is like a flash or spark to your memory and inspires all of your senses.

7. Imagine a limitless supply of coloured, powerful and inspirational light held in Archangel Metatron's hands. Metatron tells you that it is yours and it belongs back in your life. Inspiration belongs back in your relationships and your home and your career and your finances, your thoughts, your perception of yourself and your expectations of life.

8. Imagine Metatron is beginning to project the coloured light of inspiration into all of your relationships. See and feel all of your relationships becoming the colour of inspiration and coming alive and positive and full of freshness and sparkle and shine. Enjoy this experience and feeling.

9. Imagine the coloured light of inspiration is spreading outwards and covering a wider area now. It is now reaching your friends and all those that you come into contact with. It is reaching all of the situations in your life which involve other people. Inspiration is reaching your opportunities and your ideas and your thoughts. It is reaching your home, your career your working environment, your projects and your goals.

10. Archangel Metatron would like you to know that your inspiration is imprinted in the Universal mind. The Universe will provide you with inspiration which appears in all parts of your life. Inspiration will reach you through people and conversations and thoughts and ideas and feelings and emotions. The Universe will provide you with inspiration in your daily life. The Universe and the Angels will provide you with your colour and encourage you to bring this colour into your life in ways that remind you of who you are, and that is possible for you.

11. Thank Archangel Metatron for helping you to become inspired and motivated by the possibilities your life now holds.

An Angelic Card Exercise for You to Enjoy

Take a moment to read about Oracle Card Reading on page 7 before you begin.

As you have seen in Chapter 8, Archangel Metatron will inspire, he will motivate and he will provide you with the final push you need to complete a task, conquer a challenge or to finally take the positive action required in your life. It is now time to ask Archangel Metatron to provide you with his guidance and further insight through Oracle Cards.

Take your Oracle Cards in your hands and fill them with Love and all that Love means to you. Allow your cards to become warmed by your hands. Gently shuffle your cards and take your time and enjoy your connection with them. Anticipate clarity and Love from your cards; expect them to help you and they will.

When you are ready, ask the Archangel Metatron:

'Archangel Metatron, please provide me with your loving guidance'

Now choose a card for each of the questions below.

Note down the cards as you choose them and what you feel that they are conveying to you.

1. What is it that Archangel Metatron would like to communicate to me today?

2. How can I feel more inspired and motivated by my life?

3. How can I identify the areas of my life in which I need to take positive action?

4. How can I release any issues which prevent me from taking positive action in my life?

And when you have finished, thank Archangel Metatron for his help by simply saying 'Thank you'.

Archangel Metatron

My Thoughts, Feelings and Requests

This is the very special place for you to record your thoughts and feelings. Use this very special place to ask the Angels to help you with anything which you become aware of or would like to ask for, as you move through the chapters of this book.

Chapter Nine

Your Guardian Angel

Chapter Nine

Your Guardian Angel

By the end of this chapter you will:

- ♥ Have called your Guardian Angel to be with you with an Angelic Invocation

- ♥ Understand how your Guardian Angel can help you to improve your life

- ♥ Have experienced the unconditional love of your Guardian Angel

- ♥ Have received your Guardian Angel's further guidance and advice with Oracle Cards

Your Guardian Angel Invocation

Take a moment to read about invocations on page 5 before you begin.

It's time to connect with the Angelic Realm now and to call your Guardian Angel to be with you. So, close your eyes and give yourself permission for this experience.

Now, take some relaxing breaths and gently focus your intention and full expectation upon connecting with your Guardian Angel.

It is your intention and expectation to connect with your Guardian Angel which will allow your channel of Angelic communication to become open.

And now ask your Guardian Angel to be with you.

Your Guardian Angel is with you right now.

Open your heart to your Guardian Angel's safe, secure and loving aura.

Feel with all of your senses and see in your mind's eye, the pure white light of your Guardian Angel's central heart light.

Ask your Guardian Angel to surround you with their unconditional love and ask your Guardian Angel to direct it to the parts of you which need to need to feel more loved and appreciated. Do that now.

Now spend some time, becoming more familiar with your Guardian Angel's energy.

Ask your Guardian Angel to help you to recognise their energy every time they are near you.

Ask that your Guardian Angel stay with you throughout this Chapter.

And so it is.

Well Done! Whether this is the first time, 50th time or the millionth time you have connected with your Guardian Angel, acknowledge and appreciate your experience and know that your relationship with your Guardian Angel is forever.

How Will You Experience Your Guardian Angel's Presence?

Remember from the beginning of this book, that there are many different ways of communicating with the Angels and in this case with your Guardian Angel. Some people will *feel* their Guardian Angel's energy, others may *see* their Guardian Angel's pure white central light, and there are those who will even see the individual colours of their Guardian Angel's bands. There are those who will *hear* their Guardian Angel's guidance or be told by their Guardian Angel that he or she is with them, or it may be that you just *know* that your Guardian Angel is present. Honour and value your communication channel with your Guardian Angel and know that it is perfect for you.

Whichever way you experience your Guardian Angel's energy, your awareness may be very subtle at first. In the beginning, you may even think that you are imagining what you are feeling. Lots of people question their initial experiences or push away the delicate gentleness of the first steps with their Guardian Angel. I encourage you to accept how good it feels and focus on all the ways you can accept more of your Guardian Angel's unconditional love for you. Ask your Guardian Angel to help you to experience their presence in many different ways – and they will.

You may begin to notice your Guardian Angel's presence with a beautiful white feather appearing. You might feel drawn towards meditations to lift your vibration. You might begin to notice repeated numbers and signs as you go about your day. You might find yourself wanting to explore new interests or discover new activities that bring you joy. Whatever you experience, enjoy and accept it, no matter how small you consider it to be. Your attention to and acceptance of your growing awareness of your Guardian Angel will see it develop beautifully over time. Your heart-centred intention to connect with your Guardian Angel will see your relationship become stronger and clearer every day.

How Can My Guardian Angel Help Me?

Your Guardian Angel is the Angel of True Life Purpose and embodies the qualities of each of your life purpose strengths, gifts and talents. Your Guardian Angel is waiting to help you to find and follow your life purpose path and live the true purpose you were born to experience.

Know that *you have a meaningful contribution to make in our world.*

Your Guardian Angel reassures you that you are loved, even when you feel lost or lonely. Your Guardian Angel encourages you to see the value of your unique strengths and the meaningful contribution you can make in the world when you release your fear of failure.

Allowing Love

Your Guardian Angel will help you to allow more love into your life. Your heart centre is the loving and sacred space within you from which love can flourish and grow. Your Guardian Angel will help you to connect with the energy of your beautiful heart centre. Each time you do, your heart centre becomes more beautiful and light-filled as it gently awakens to your Guardian Angel's love.

Take a moment: *Take a few minutes now to ask your Guardian Angel to help you to allow more love into your life. Close your eyes, place your hand over your heart centre and ask your Guardian Angel to fill you with beautiful light and gently awaken your heart centre to allow more love.*

Connecting Your Guardian Angel

Your Guardian Angel has been with you from the very moment you were conceived and will remain with you for your entire lifetime. Connecting with your Guardian Angel is something you may have wanted to do without realising. The feeling of wanting to connect with your Guardian Angel can show up in subtle ways. For some, there is a continuous sense that something is missing, even when there seems to be so much to be grateful for. For others, there is a feeling that they are here for something more, even though they do not know what that could possibly be. Often there is a yearning inside to live a life you just can't put your finger on.

Conditioning Prevents Connection

Your Guardian Angel's presence never wavers, it is our awareness of their presence that fades with time. It is a sadness that from the moment we are born our memory of who we are and who we came to be, begins to fade. The conditioning we experience in our society can create a barrier between us and our Guardian Angels. We are convinced from an early age, that the only true reality is that which can be seen and accepted by all. Yet we are all born with a Guardian Angel by our side.

Many of us felt or knew our Guardian Angel's presence as a child. The young child smiling and laughing in their crib when no one can be seen, knows their Guardian Angel. The wisdom in a newborn baby's eyes reflects the knowledge of their Guardian Angel.

The struggles of the physical world and the conditioning we experience as we grow, cause the connection between us and our Guardian Angel to fade a little more with each day of our physical existence.

Taking the First Step with Your Guardian Angel

You may have felt a longing to connect with your Guardian Angel for some time, but didn't know how to or where to go to find out. To truly connect with your Guardian Angel you must be willing to approach life in a new way. You may feel like you are trying to *meet* your Guardian Angel when they are already with you. Until you take steps to welcome your Guardian Angel into your life, knowing your Guardian Angel is almost impossible. To truly connect, you must learn to allow your Guardian Angel's love into your heart. Your connection with your Guardian Angel can begin when you welcome them into your life and ask them to help you to live your life together.

Open your heart and say *"Dear Guardian Angel, I welcome you into my life and I am ready to live life together with you."*

Connecting in Your Daily Life

Your Guardian Angel will help you to connect with them in your daily life. You may connect with your Guardian Angel in the shower, in dreams, finding white feathers, or being shown repeated numbers or signs as you go through your day.

Going on walks in nature, journaling and doing things that you enjoy are all ways to develop your connection with your Guardian Angel and allow your Guardian Angel to begin to communicate with you too.

Your trust will grow and your connection become stronger as you allow their unconditional love to guide and support you. Your Guardian Angel will guide you through the validation of your thoughts and feelings and help you to make the best choices for yourself.

Your Guardian Angel is always helping you to find and follow your life purpose path. When you do what you love and share the gifts you were born with, your Guardian Angel can guide you to your true purpose in life.

Your Guardian Angel's Name

Your Guardian Angel has a completely unique name and a meaning that connects you to your true purpose in life. Your Guardian Angel has never been human. They are not, nor ever have been male or female. They are energy, without gender and have never held a physical form. Your Guardian Angel will connect with you as a male or female energy and their name is given in order to help you to connect with them within the context of your physical world understanding of relationships.

When you know your Guardian Angel's name you have a precise message about your life purpose. Your Guardian Angel's name carries a tiny piece of your life purpose and provides an instant connection and a highly significant validation of who they are and by connection, who you are.

Your Guardian Angel's Number

Your Guardian Angel has a special number that has important personal significance. Your Guardian Angel's number is within the range from four to eight and relates to an over-arching character theme of your life purpose. Your Guardian Angel's special number is shown as their number of bands.

Here are descriptions of the Guardian Angel special numbers:

Fours are pure work and business-focused individuals who are laser-focused on making ideas into reality.

Fives are freedom-seeking lovers of change who love to motivate and inspire others to get the most from their lives.

Sixes are supportive and empowering champions of others who naturally give themselves to helping others.

Sevens are entranced by the journey of discovery, research and exploration and love to go on adventures in life.

Eights are true harmony creators who naturally seek to unify, bring together and provide space for alternative perspectives to be heard.

You may like to consider each of the special Guardian Angel numbers and enjoy discovering yours by the number that speaks to you most.

Your Guardian Angel Embodies Your Life Purpose

Your Guardian Angel embodies your unique life-purpose strengths within their beautifully coloured bands. Each of your Guardian Angel's colours embodies a personal strength and the unique quality of one of your life-purpose strengths. Your Guardian Angel's presence is always radiating the colours and qualities of your life purpose strengths and keeping their promise to guide you to your true purpose.

It is my experience that a large number of spiritual souls don't recognize or understand what their special qualities and strengths are. It feels uncomfortable to sit down and think about themselves in that way. Instead, many have spent more time trying to fix their shortcomings rather than developing their strengths. All too often, this results in spiritual souls struggling through their whole life with their unique strengths untapped.

Finding and developing your strengths is a simple but powerful step that is done more easily than you might expect. Being willing to open yourself up and to ask your Guardian Angel to help you to develop your strengths is a valuable endeavour that will lead you to live your true purpose in life.

Something essential to remember is that you will only find your true purpose in life by doing what you love to do and are good at doing. The key is identifying the unique life purpose strengths you were born with and understanding precisely how to apply them to your life. Your connection with your Guardian Angel and allowing their love into your life is the way to tap into your unique strengths and, together, have the best possible life imaginable.

Chapter 9 – Visualisation

Connecting with Your Guardian Angel

The purpose of this visualisation is to help you to accept your Guardian Angel's love. Your Guardian Angel will surround you with their cocoon of love and light and raise your vibration and the vibration of everything around you.

Every time you connect with your Guardian Angel you become more charged with their love and light and your vibration is increased.

You can connect with your Guardian Angel for a few moments every day at work, at home and even as you walk, to raise your vibration and become charged with your Guardian Angel's light.

1. Sit quietly with your eyes closed and relax your body. Place your hands gently in your lap with your palms facing upwards. Imagine your whole body relaxing and becoming physically comfortable.

2. Give this Angelic experience to yourself as a precious gift of love. Give yourself this gift of love which will fill you with light and raise your vibration.

3. Become aware of your breath and allow your focus to gently come to rest with your own rhythm and notice how comfortable it is. Allow yourself to enjoy full inhalations of breath and feel your heart reaching upwards to the Angels as you do.

4. Call upon your guardian angel, the Angel of True Life Purpose to be with you and know that your call is responded to immediately. Your Guardian Angel is with you now.

5. Imagine your guardian angel's beautiful shimmering radiant white light reaching you. Greet and warmly welcome your Guardian Angel and invite your Guardian Angel closer. Peace, love and joy surround you.

6. Imagine your Guardian Angel's light forming a cocoon of pure white light all around you and sense how this cocoon of pure white light raises the vibration of you and everything around you.

7. Now call in more light and invite your Guardian Angel to radiate beautiful white light through your whole being and increase your vibration.

8. Imagine your heart centre begin to gently awaken and glow with the radiant pure white light that is reaching you. Feel the light from your heart centre increasing your feelings of love and raising your vibration.

9. Enjoy this beautiful experience of *connection* with your Guardian Angel. Allow your heart centre to become charged with your Guardian Angel's pure white light and feeling more connected, more loved and more loving then ever before.

10. Return to the room feeling charged with love and your heart centre filled with the unconditional love and light of your guardian angel.

11. Thank your Guardian Angel for helping you to gently awaken your heart centre and receive unconditional love and light.

An Angelic Card Exercise for You to Enjoy

Take a moment to read about Oracle Card Reading on page 7 before you begin.

As you have seen in Chapter 9, working with your Guardian Angel will help you to find and follow your life purpose path. Your Guardian Angel will help you in many ways to discover the meaningful contribution you are here to make in the world. It is now time to ask your Guardian Angel to provide you with guidance and further insight through Oracle Cards.

Take your Oracle Cards in your hands and fill them with Love and all that Love means to you. Allow your cards to become warmed by your hands. Gently shuffle your cards and take your time and enjoy your connection with them. Anticipate clarity and Love from your cards; expect them to help you and they will.

When you are ready, ask your Guardian Angel:

'Dear Guardian Angel, please provide me with your loving guidance'

Now choose a card for each of the questions below.

Note down the cards as you choose them and what you feel that they are conveying to you.

1. What is it that my Guardian Angel would like to communicate to me today?

2. How can I allow more of your love into my life?

3. How can I *identify* my unique life purpose strengths?

4. How can I *release* any blocks to discovering my true purpose in life?

And when you have finished, thank your Guardian Angel for their help by simply saying 'Thank you'.

Your Guardian Angel

My Thoughts, Feelings and Requests

This is the very special place for you to record your thoughts and feelings. Use this very special place to ask the Angels to help you with anything which you become aware of or would like to ask for, as you move through the chapters of this book.

I Can Help You

I can help you to connect with the Angels in many different ways. Have a look at my website: **www.angels-with-ros.com** for lots of opportunities to learn more about Archangels and Guardian Angels.

I offer:
- ❤ Guardian Angel Readings
- ❤ Guardian Angel Courses
- ❤ Oracle Card Courses
- ❤ 1:1 Mentored Channelling Programs

You can see my NEW book The Channel of Clarity Method here:
- ❤ www.channelofclarity.com

Take a look at:
- ❤ www.angels-with-ros.com
- ❤ www.channelofclarity.com
- ❤ www.youtube.com/@RosPlace

I look forward to seeing you there ☺

With love Ros and Tressarn xxx

Visualisations

All 9 of the Angelic Visualisations from this book are available for you on my website:

www.angels-with-ros.com/book1

Each Angelic Visualisation recording will bring you even closer to the Archangels and enhance your Angelic connection for years and years to come.

You will benefit from:

❤ Professional Studio Recordings

❤ The Complete Version of Each Visualisation

❤ Feeling Immersed in the Angelic Realm

❤ Dedicated Time for Your Angelic Connection

❤ Developing Your Angelic Relationships

❤ Stronger Personal Guidance & Intuition

266 | Lightworking with Angels Book 1

Lightworking with Angels Book 2

RELEASED 2023

'**Lightworking with Angels**' Book 2 has been written to explain how to bring the Archangels into your life in a more advanced and powerful way. Book 2 will sit beautifully on top of the foundation created in Book 1 and really increase and enhance your Angelic connection.

It will reintroduce you to the Archangels Michael, Gabriel, Raphael and Metatron. It will show you different aspects and dimensions to work with in your life. You will also connect once again with your Guardian Angel and discover more about your unique life purpose strengths.

Book 2 will introduce you to the Archangels Uriel and Jophiel, which will broaden and strengthen your Angelic knowledge and expertise.

💙 Uriel and Jophiel are waiting to meet you

Printed in Great Britain
by Amazon